NEW ENGLAND FAIRIES

A HISTORY OF THE LITTLE PEOPLE

OF THE HILLS AND FORESTS

ANDREW WARBURTON

THE
History
PRESS

Published by The History Press
Charleston, SC
www.historypress.com

Copyright © 2024 by Andrew Warburton
All rights reserved

First published 2024

Manufactured in the United States

ISBN 9781467158206

Library of Congress Control Number: 2024936983

For my mother, Mary Hemmings,
who gave me a love of stories

CONTENTS

ACKNOWLEDGEMENTS

Many people contributed to the research contained in this book, and I'm indebted to folklorists and authors who've drawn attention to New England stories about fairies, including Peter Muise, whose blog *New England Folklore* is an excellent resource; Joseph Strange; Chris Woodyard; Erik Ofgang; Richard Holmes; and Joseph Citro. I'd like to thank Ann Price and author John Cilio of Sherman, Connecticut, for helping me uncover the truth about Perry Boney; Janet Kerschner at the Theosophical Society for sending me photos of Dora Kunz; Charles and Barbara Adams for allowing me to visit their art collection and photograph Tomah Joseph's artwork; Sam Baltrusis, without whose guidance and example this book would not have happened; Michael Kinsella at The History Press for believing in this project and Abigail Fleming for her excellent editing; Ray Mckenna for his *Federal Hill Irish* blog, his work uncovering his ancestors' fairy lore and his permission to use a photograph of his great-grandmother Ellen Carson; Rachel Sayet, whose master's thesis was invaluable for my understanding of Mohegan folklore; the helpful guides at the Tantaquidgeon Museum; Simon Young and the Fairy Investigation Society for access to the Fairy Censuses; Lorén Spears at the Tomaquag Museum; Christopher Packard for improving my knowledge of Maine folklore; Julia Ospina, park manager at Button Bay State Park; the Aquinnah Cultural Center; and Tracey Kry at Mount Holyoke College Archives and Special Collections. Lastly, I would like to thank Dr. Mary Hemmings for her excellent reading and editing skills while looking at drafts and John Grillo for his constant support.

INTRODUCTION

What is a fairy? A tiny winged being that flutters among the flowerbeds at the bottom of the garden? Or a powerful spirit living underground or far away in the hills and forests? Diverse types of fairies appear in folklore, some shining and beautiful, others spectacularly ugly like the Scottish redcap with its leathery skin and prominent fangs. While fairies are sometimes described as spirits, many stories from Ireland and Great Britain depict them as having physical bodies capable of being injured or killed. Here I use the term *fairy* to refer to any humanoid being that possesses magical powers and lives among us or in the natural world. Although I sometimes call fairies *Little People*, this term was historically a euphemism—a way to cast supernatural beings that might otherwise appear frightening in a more sympathetic and familiar light. This means the fairies described in this book are sometimes tall and often threatening.

The six northeastern states known collectively as New England—Connecticut, Maine, Massachusetts, New Hampshire, Rhode Island and Vermont—are arguably the perfect location to investigate American fairies. Being where many of the earliest British colonies in North America were founded, these states were also among the first to witness a flowering of European fairy lore in the New World. Between the seventeenth and twentieth centuries, the region welcomed a huge diversity of immigrants, creating a melting pot of folkloric influences. As will become clear from the following chapters—one for each state—British, Irish, French and Native American fairies all coexist in the region.

The topic of fairies hasn't always been popular in New England. The Puritans who left Europe in the seventeenth century to establish colonies in North America had little room for the "fairy faith" in their strictly Calvinist worldview. Those early Americans saw the world in terms of the "saved" and the "damned," and anything tending to complicate that picture was probably considered a distraction at best or diabolical at worst. Unfortunately for the Gentle Folk of British and Irish folklore, their existence fell outside the dichotomy of good and evil, occupying a gray cosmological space, which troubled the average Puritan. Battling to survive in a harsh new land, the pious early Americans lacked the frivolity and mirth to tell a good fairy story.

One explanation of the fairies' troublesome nature can be found in the folklorist Enys Tregarthen's claim that the Cornish of South West England called their pixies "Eve's unwashed children." The term refers to a folkloric "origin story" in which God visited Eve one day while she was busily bathing her children and asked to see how many she had. Embarrassed by her unwashed children, Eve hid them from God's sight and showed him only the clean ones. As punishment for her deception, God doomed the "unclean children" to remain hidden in the earth. Becoming fairies, they fled into the hills and forests, where they lived out an existence having little to do with humans and nothing to do with religion. (They couldn't abide the sight of the cross and hated the touch of holy water.) The old saying goes, they were "neither good enough for heaven nor evil enough for hell."

The story's complexity, admitting no simple dichotomy of good and evil, goes some way toward explaining why the rather rigid Puritans left the fairy faith behind them when they arrived on America's shores. A character in Nathaniel Hawthorne's *The Scarlet Letter* expresses the Puritan antipathy to magical folklore when he refers to those "naughty elves or fairies whom we thought to have left behind us, with other relics of Papistry, in merry old England." The implication is that England, despite having thrown off the influence of Roman Catholicism, is still suffused with irrational and superstitious thinking, the fairy faith being one example. Here in America, we don't believe in such things. As the children of Boston's public schools sang on Boston Common during that city's Water Celebration in 1848, "No fairies in the *Mayflower* came."

Nevertheless, the old Puritan disbelief couldn't stop fairies from arriving on these shores forever. Other immigrants, less rigid in their beliefs and more attached to Old World folklore, brought a wider range of stories with them. They established fairy superstitions in communities throughout New

Louis Rhead's depiction of the famous English fairy Puck from Shakespeare's *A Midsummer Night's Dream. Public domain.*

England, including the English of Marblehead, Massachusetts, with their mischievous pixies; the French Canadians of Maine, with their *lutins* and *feux follets*; and the Irish of Rhode Island, with their banshees.

AMERICAN IMMIGRANT FAIRIES

Until recently, New England fairy lore remained a largely unexplored field of study. Although folklorists have written extensively about Native American Little People traditions in New England, European immigrant stories have often been overlooked. In comparison, evidence that fairy belief existed in regions of North America adjacent to New England in the late nineteenth or early twentieth century, including Nova Scotia and Appalachia, is plentiful. Folklorist Katharine Briggs, for instance, shared two tales about American immigrant fairies in her *An Encyclopedia of Fairies*. The stories, collected in the 1920s, provide a taste of the types of tales we'll encounter in this book. The elderly pair who recounted the tales likely resided in Kentucky's Southern Appalachian Mountains, quite far from New England. However, the ethnic groups who settled in Southern Appalachia, including the Scots Irish, also settled in parts of New England, meaning their stories share many characteristics with the material of the Northeast. I share them here because they provide a wider context for the New England fairy folklore presented in this book.

The first of Briggs's stories, told by an old man of British descent called Tom Field, invokes the notion of "elf-shot." The idea, common in British folklore, is that elves, seen or unseen, shoot humans and animals with arrows to make them sick. Riding home one evening on his horse, Tom came upon a "red-headed fairy no bigger than a tiny child" and "a number of others dancing and whirling at a distance." The old man watched the fairies until the red-headed straggler flew off to join the rest. At that moment, Tom noticed something hurtling through the air toward him, and his horse became suddenly lame. He went home and waited until the morning, but the horse remained sick. It was only when he returned to the haunted spot and discovered the arrowhead the Little People had flung at him that his horse became "free of fairy enchantment."

Another story, told by an old woman called Granny Caudill (also of British descent), involves the motif, frequently encountered in Old World fairy lore, of a girl "called into a fairy hill by the music" and dancing the night away. In the morning, when the girl wished to leave the enchanted domain, the fairies told her she could do so only if she baked all "the meal in the bin." Although it looked to the girl as if she'd soon complete her task, she could never quite bring the work to an end. (Fairies, apparently, love to set impossible tasks.) It was only through the assistance of another human captive, who showed her how to bake the meal, that she managed to finish the job.

Both stories are examples of what Briggs identified as Scottish lore infiltrating North America, and although they were shared in Southern Appalachia, the evidence suggests New Englanders told similar stories. Scottish fairy lore, in particular, planted deep roots in the soil of New Hampshire, as we'll see.

A FAIRY VISIONARY IN NEW ENGLAND

The most thorough and committed attempt to describe a real-life New England fairy can be found in the theosophical writings of Dora van Gelder Kunz, a Dutchwoman who immigrated to America in 1927. A seer of fairies since she was five years old, Kunz was a kind of David Attenborough of fairyland: she studied her subjects in detail and filled a whole book (*The Real World of Fairies*) with her descriptions. Unlike some time-honored European folklore in which fairies appear to be flesh-and-blood beings prone to sickness and death, Kunz's work took a more spiritual approach, asserting that fairies are beings of "pure feeling." Such ideas reflected her theosophical beliefs and conformed to the earlier, Victorian depiction of fairies as beautiful floating spirits mainly concerned with helping plants grow.

One of Kunz's main goals was to devise an anatomical description of a fairy, and so she set about examining what she called "a common woods or garden fairy," or, more specifically, "a green fairy of the New England woods." The ubiquity of this type of fairy in the woods of the Northeast made an analysis of one particularly easy, she said. Regarding the appearance of such a fairy, she claimed they were about "six inches tall, with a slender body and a head which is rather larger in proportion to his body than is common among adult human beings." Although they do have a physical form, their body is made of a state of matter "more like a vapor than anything else we know of in our world." They are closer in form to a "cloud" of emerald-green gas, a "thinner" aura of the same matter surrounding it "on all sides." Unlike gases known to human scientists, the fairy body is "vital matter," composed

Dora Kunz, who saw many fairies in the woods while staying at a friend's cabin in New Hampshire. *The Theosophical Society in America.*

of pure feeling, and its movements are expressions of its wishes and desires. This means that when a fairy wishes to go somewhere, it floats there almost immediately. Although the fairy has a gaseous anatomy, it does have vague structures within it similar to capillaries, veins and arteries, which carry life throughout its body, while a "golden light" of pure life shines where its heart should be. One finds such fairies, Kunz wrote, wherever plants grow: they constantly tend to plants' well-being by attuning their natural vibration to the vibration of the plants, thereby bestowing energy upon them.

Although Kunz's fairies are often quite different from the beings mentioned in the folklore of this land, her descriptions may prove interesting to those wishing to understand various aspects of fairy existence. If the reader finds her ideas helpful, he or she may wish to keep them in mind when reading the stories that follow. Otherwise, one might view them as the subjective revelations of a fairy seer rather than an objective look at New England fairies.

One might also wish to read Kunz's fairy writings alongside the work of another fairy-enchanted New Englander, Louisa May Alcott, who wrote a collection of children's stories, *Flower Fables*, focused on the relationship between fairies and flowers, while living in Concord, Massachusetts. Although Alcott's fairies are allegorical in nature, they point to a transcendental relationship with nature that's in fact quite similar to Kunz's work. Alcott was a protégé of Henry David Thoreau and visited the woods near Walden Pond, which at that time went by the name of Fairyland. (Yes, New England has its very own fairyland, now called Hapgood Wright Town Forest.) There Thoreau was said to have pointed to a dew-bedecked cobweb and described it as a "fairy's handkerchief" tossed into the woods.

NATIVE AMERICAN TRADITIONS

The most ancient fairy folklore in New England comprises the various Native American traditions. These are also among the most abundant, detailed and colorful traditions. While European immigrant stories are scattered throughout New England, the Native American stories suffuse the land, placing fairylike beings in every corner of the region. For this reason, they occupy an important place in this book. Although Katharine Briggs speculated that the Algonquian tribes may have received their Little People stories from the Jesuits who evangelized them in the early seventeenth

Little People legends are found in many Native American traditions. Illustration from Mabel Powers's *Stories The Iroquois Tell Their Children*. *Public domain.*

century, the stories themselves are so rich and unique and are peopled with so many beings unheard of in European lore, they appear to represent an independent tradition.

The first thing to remember is that it's important to distinguish between the stories of different nations. Although some cultural exchange took place between different tribes—the Mohegans, for example, may have learned about the Little People from the Wampanoag—each tradition must be understood in the context of the tribe's territory and heritage.

For the purpose of this book, Native American Little People traditions can be divided into two camps: the stories of northern New England, on the one hand, and the stories of southern New England on the other. In the north are the peoples of the Wabanaki Confederacy, a confederation of tribes with cultural similarities. These tribes include the Passamaquoddy and Penobscot (or Eastern Abenaki) in Maine, with their water fairies, dwarves and Little People familiars; and the Western Abenaki in Vermont, with their swamp spirits and Little People residing in rivers. In the south are the Mohegans in Connecticut, the Narragansett in Rhode Island and the Wampanoag in Massachusetts. All the Native American peoples of the North and South are ancestrally related, preserve variations of the Algonquian language and share a fair amount of folklore, often focused on interactions with the Little People. More will be explained about the various traditions of the Native American peoples in the relevant chapters.

THE FAIRY CENSUSES

A word about the Fairy Censuses of 2014–2017 and 2017–2023, which I refer to throughout this book. Carried out by the academic Simon Young and the Fairy Investigation Society, the censuses invited respondents from all over the world to describe their fairy beliefs and experiences. The sections on North America are obviously particularly relevant to this book because they feature the testimony of respondents from five of the six New England states: Connecticut, Maine, Massachusetts, New Hampshire and Vermont. As well as asking respondents to explain their beliefs and experiences in detail, the censuses asked them to provide general information such as the time of day when the encounter occurred, the state of mind they happened to be in and whether they'd been taking any mind-altering substances. At the end of each of the five chapters mentioned above, I provide a summary of the census findings, a brief interpretation of the entries and some thoughts on the nature of the fairy faith in the given state. I invite the reader to compare and contrast the modern fairy sightings found in the censuses with the more traditional stories found elsewhere in the book.

Unfortunately, the issue of space has prevented me from drawing on both censuses exhaustively, and I therefore focus mainly on summarizing the census of 2014–2017. Where material from the first census is lacking, as in the case of Vermont, I supplement the information with narratives drawn from the census of 2017–2023. Respondents from Rhode Island do not appear in either census.

1

CONNECTICUT

Traveling in the springtime along Connecticut's highways in search of fairy-frequented locations and their associated lore, one appears to be moving through an endless forest, untouched except for intersecting roads and a scattering of towns and cities. Lush green sprawls in every direction—from the state's eastern regions, home to that benevolent fairy being the *makiawisug*, to the western regions closer to New York, where Middlebury boasts a desolate "Little People's Village" in an out-of-the-way woodland, and where the enchanted town of Sherman, nestled in the woody hills, once embraced a real-life fairy (if the "broken telephone" of twentieth-century legends are to be believed).

I started my research for this book in the east, on the rocky summit of Mohegan Hill, where some of New England's most ancient fairy folklore originated: the stories of the Mohegan Tribe and their encounters with the Little People of the forest, called the makiawisug. I quickly learned that Mohegan fairy lore is inseparable from the person of Fidelia Fielding, a late tribal elder who shared much of what we know about the makiawisug with researchers in 1903. Fielding was a veritable seer: not only did she believe in the Little People, but she was also said to have communicated with them face to face. Here, I give a summary of Mohegan beliefs about the makiawisug and recount the major stories.

My research then took me west to Sherman in the vicinity of Candlewood Lake to investigate the legend of Perry Boney, a man whose life has been thoroughly mythologized since his death in 1921, from the first almost-contemporary whispers of his association with the fae to the later suggestion he might actually have been a fairy. As far as I'm aware, nobody who's ever read the legends has gone to Sherman to investigate them, so that's exactly what I did. There I met a woman in her nineties whose grandparents knew Perry well, and she filled me in on the truth of the matter. The facts I uncovered are, of course, more mundane than the legends suggest, but does this necessarily rule out every connection Perry may have had with the fairies? Read on to find out.

Finally, I reached the town of Middlebury and a decrepit, abandoned collection of fairy houses known locally as the Little People's Village, a location steeped in distressing lore but with an apparently prosaic backstory. If the story of this little attraction is so ordinary, ruling out the supernatural, why do those who visit the location—myself included—feel such inexplicable dread?

THE LITTLE PEOPLE OF MOHEGAN HILL

Below the Yantic Falls in rural eastern Connecticut, the Yantic River flows placidly through the town of Norwich toward Mohegan Hill, ancient home of the Native American Mohegan Tribe. One day in the late 1700s, a young Mohegan girl, canoeing along the Yantic with her mother and father, caught sight of chaotic movement among the pine trees on the riverbank: crowds of little men were running beside the water.

"Don't look at those little men," the girl's mother said hurriedly, "or they'll point their fingers at you and you won't be able to see them anymore."

Although the girl listened carefully to her mother and made sure not to look at them directly, she'd never forget the magical sight of those tiny men racing through the trees. It was her first encounter with that tribe of Little People whom the Mohegans call the makiawisug—fairylike beings of a secretive but generally benevolent nature said to live beneath the woods and rocks of Mohegan Hill. Many years later, when the girl was old and gray-haired, she would share the story with her grandchildren, who in turn would share it with their grandchildren.

Most of what we know about this fantastical race of beings comes from the oral storytelling of Fidelia Fielding, a Mohegan elder and last fluent speaker of the Mohegan language, who, before she died at the age of eighty in 1908, sat down with anthropologist Frank Speck and recorded many fascinating

The Yantic Falls above the Yantic River where a Mohegan girl saw the Little People running through the woods in the eighteenth century. *Author's photo*.

stories drawn from Mohegan folklore, translated for her by interpreters. The girl in the Yantic River story was actually Fidelia's grandmother's grandmother, and everything she shared in her interview with Speck, she learned from her tribe's elder women, their memories stretching back into the distant past when European settlers had not yet arrived in this land.

We know from Fidelia's recollections that the makiawisug were as small as young children, lived underground and had an ambivalent relationship with humans. In the Mohegan language, their name meant "whip-poor-will moccasins" because they wore shoes made of moccasin flowers and emerged in the evening when the song of the whip-poor-will bird filled the air. Although they were credited with teaching the Mohegans how to grow corn and make medicine, they weren't always magnanimous or protective beings. They often expected gifts from the Mohegans in response to a particular need, and food was usually the gift of choice. Fidelia claimed the Mohegans saw them sometimes at the doors of their longhouses or wigwams where they'd come in search of food. "You must always give them what they wanted," she said, "for if you didn't they would point at you, then, while you couldn't see them, they would take what they wanted."

The Mohegans offered food to the Little People for many years, a practice that eventually transformed into a spiritual ritual of leaving baskets of corn and tobacco on the hillside. After sunset, when the whip-poor-will's call filled the woods, the Little People put on their soft pink moccasin-flower shoes and emerged from their hideouts among the rocks of Mohegan Hill to collect their gifts. The Mohegans believed that if they were good to the Little People, the Little People would nurture and protect the tribe. According to one tour guide at the Mohegans' Tantaquidgeon Museum, this belief remains alive even among contemporary tribe members and their children.

Although it was a rare event for a Mohegan to encounter a Little Person in the flesh, one fairly detailed story about a tribe member's interactions with the makiawisug has survived. Fidelia learned the story from her grandmother, suggesting its roots are entirely Mohegan. Nevertheless, the events described bear a striking resemblance to European tales of fairy visitations and abductions. It also demonstrates the level of respect and care the Mohegans showed for their otherworldly neighbors.

Opposite: Fidelia Fielding, last fluent speaker of the Mohegan language, who preserved many Mohegan traditions for posterity, including Little People stories. *Public domain.*

Right: An offering basket in which food and tobacco would be left for the Little People, found in the Mohegan Tantaquidgeon Museum. *Author's photo.*

The events occurred one stormy night long before the arrival of the European settlers. A man and woman who lived on Mohegan Hill heard a knock at their longhouse door. Upon opening the door, the woman saw what at first appeared to be a little boy waiting on the threshold. He asked if she'd come away with him and tend to a woman he'd left lying sick at home. Going with the boy, she soon realized he was actually a little man, and after traveling a long way through the blustery wind and rain, they came to an illuminated house where a little woman was found convalescing on a pile of skins. The woman remained with the fairy pair for a long time and cared diligently for the little woman until she was quite well. Then, after loading her with gifts, the couple permitted her to return to Mohegan Hill. Her departure was contingent on one condition: she must cover her eyes with a "piece of skin" and allow the man to guide her footsteps home. When she finally arrived at Mohegan Hill and removed the skin from her eyes, the little man was nowhere to be seen.

One curious characteristic of this story is its similarity to Irish and British fairy lore. A common feature of European tales is the notion that Little People visit humans to enlist help in caring for a member of their race. Fairies sometimes snatch men's wives and carry them off to fairyland or abduct a mortal woman to act as midwife to a fairy baby. The Mohegan story differs from those tales in that the human woman goes willingly. However, the fairies' obscure location and the nursing of a magical being are found in both. How similarities arose between the two traditions is unclear, especially when the English Puritans and Dutch Calvinists who first arrived on these shores were hardly likely to bring the fairy faith with them.

Sadly, the makiawisug's magical presence on Mohegan Hill didn't last forever, and Mohegan belief in their existence fluctuated. Having lived alongside the tribe since long before the Europeans arrived in North America, the Little People began to disappear sometime after the English settled in the land. It was almost as if they'd "died out," said Fidelia, and those who remained "kept away" and "lived way back in the woods." Although Fidelia remained a firm believer in the Little People as late as the twentieth century, her fellow tribe members, at that point, rarely believed in them. They no longer reported sightings of the Little People on Mohegan Hill or left them baskets of food. The European settlers' arrival seemed to have changed the relationship between the Mohegans and the Little People, a change summed up in Fidelia's melancholy statement that "folks saw more things in the woods than they do nowadays."

Nevertheless, the Mohegans' relationship with the makiawisug persisted, and despite the decline in Little People beliefs, contemporary Mohegans such as Rachel Sayet attest to the survival of Little People stories in the present day. A distant relative of Fidelia, Sayet learned about the makiawisug from her grandmother and aunts as a little girl on Mohegan Hill. "We would sit at their kitchen table and drink tea while they would tell me stories," she wrote. During these gatherings, Sayet heard the warning, often mentioned in stories about fairies, of not speaking too much about the Little People for fear of offending them. She also learned about the practice of leaving "baskets of tobacco and corn" for them in the woods, as well as stories about the deity-like medicine woman Granny Squannit, legendary leader of the makiawisug.

I mention Granny Squannit here because she's perhaps the most important fairylike being in Mohegan and Wampanoag folklore. According to ancient stories, she lived alongside the Mohegans many years ago and helped the tribe develop its distinctive way of life. As her name (which means "female

Depiction of Granny Squannit in the Mohegan Tantaquidgeon Museum. Note the eye in the middle of her forehead. *Author's photo.*

spirit") suggests, Granny Squannit is associated with the earth, medicine, and children and is sometimes described as a "woman's god." In times past, she gathered herbs from the woods to heal the Mohegans and their magical neighbors. Folklore describes her as a tribal protector, wife of the benevolent giant Maushop, and an intimidating figure who keeps her face covered with long strands of hair and who's known to come "creeping up on her hands and feet" to steal Mohegan children when they're bad. We'll hear more about Granny Squannit in the chapter on Massachusetts.

Returning to the present day, it appears the Mohegan Tribe's official belief about the Little People is that they live in seclusion on the hill and continue to protect modern-day tribe members, particularly the elders who inhabit a retirement community there. The Mohegans' attachment to the makiawisug received media attention in 2012 when the tribe opposed the development of a private housing community on Mohegan Hill, causing the plans to be scrapped. In a letter to the Department of Housing and Urban Development, the tribe stated that the land in question is home to "sacred stone piles…created by the 'Little People' who live deep within the grounds of Mohegan Hill." These stone piles, they explained, "possess powers that protect the Mohegan people from outsiders." Significantly, the tribe claimed that the Little People "still live within the ground on the Hill and continue to guard the stones," adding that modern-day "Mohegan tribal members make offerings to the 'Little People' in hopes that they will continue to protect our Tribe."

After visiting Mohegan Hill on a fact-finding mission, I can attest to the energy one feels when walking there. The thick woods littered with stones, and the sight of many old rock walls, impress on the mind a sense of ancient pathways emerging in the present. I recommend visiting the tribe's Tantaquidgeon Museum and seeing the eighteenth-century offering basket to the Little People displayed there. There's also a Granny Squannit herb garden to educate visitors about the tribe's folkloric traditions. The museum guide told me that tribe members continue to leave baskets in the woods for the Little People. They also tell their children that the makiawisug take many forms, including animals, which means they must always treat creatures with kindness in case they're one of the Little People.

Whether the Little People remain on Mohegan Hill to this day or whether they've all died out, as Fidelia Fielding suggested, is a question only the Mohegans can answer. I did, however, leave a pile of wild blueberries near the rocks, as an offering, just in case.

THE "FAIRY MAN" OF SHERMAN

I found myself in the town of Sherman looking for the truth about a "fairy man" called Perry Boney who, according to legend, lived in the early twentieth century in the mountainous Candlewood Lake region. Although modern folklorists such as Peter Muise and David Philips have written about this remarkable man, he remains a highly mysterious figure: Did he actually exist? If he did, was he a seer? Was he a victim of fairy enchantment? Did he appear out of nowhere and disappear as mysteriously as he'd come? Or was he a fairy himself, incarnate somehow in human flesh?

Surrounded by Sherman's enchanted streets with their centuries-old homes, quaint gambrel roofs and barns that totter on rickety foundations, one could almost be forgiven for believing a fairy did once live here: the beauty is fairylike indeed. But don't let the location's enchantment fool you. There's truth behind the legend of the "fairy" Perry Boney.

Folklore says that Perry lived alone at the foot of Coburn Mountain, a few miles to the south of the town. One day, as if from nowhere, he appeared in Sherman and opened a store in a haphazardly put together shack. The locals soon began calling it the World's Smallest Store because only a single adult or two children could fit inside it. When Perry fixed you with his china-blue eyes, you felt a bit like a phantom: he appeared to look right through you. It was unsettling—or amusing to some—but stranger still when he spoke in that voice, whispery as the wind when it came down sharp from the hill in winter. And when he called to his four-legged friend—a tame raccoon with rolls of fat—and fed it by hand like a trusty sheepdog, you'd be forgiven for thinking Perry was cracked.

For his face was always dirty, and his hair was unkempt, and his downright odd or otherworldly behavior—like the time he dug the foundations of a home in the middle of Coburn Cemetery—made him the butt of everyone's jokes. The children of the town were convinced the fairies had touched him. Sometimes when they played together at twilight in Greenwoods Brook, they saw Perry strolling beside the water, and they wondered if he was speaking to himself or conversing with the fairies. They'd whisper to each other, "The Wee Folk are here," and watch Perry until he moved out of sight. Was it a song or a spell he was singing? Had his eyes really shone like the pebbles in the brook? When they got home, they'd tell their parents what they'd seen: "Perry's away with the fairies!" Their parents would scold them for gossiping.

Greenwoods Brook in Sherman, where legend says Perry Boney spoke to fairies. *Author's photo*.

Even Sherman's adults began to wonder about the things they'd seen and heard: like, how did Perry make his living? Everyone had seen his store, the bits and bobs he placed on rickety shelves around the walls, and everyone was sure he sold those goods at the very same price he paid for them at the general store. So how did he ever make a profit? They knew he wasn't one for labor, and he hated hunting (animals were his only friends), so how on earth did he feed himself? Something definitely wasn't right.

One day, a hunter passed by the store and noticed the door blowing in the wind. Perry wasn't home. When the hunter returned that evening—still no Perry. The next day, just the same.

Perry had vanished and would never return, and no one seemed particularly surprised. The children said the fairies had taken him. That's what happens when you spend too long in the woods around the brook. Others said he'd returned to fairyland and wouldn't be coming back. Others said he'd died, been eaten by bears. But nobody forgot the magic, the strangeness, of Perry Boney.

Uncovering the historical facts behind the folklore of Perry Boney began with the discovery of a 1938 Connecticut guidebook and its brief reference to the former location of Perry's store on Route 37. One and one-tenth of a mile after the road crosses Quaker Brook, a "half-timbered, Swiss chalet-style home" now occupies the site, said the guidebook. Those who've repeated the legend of Perry Boney have apparently never checked if the directions were right.

On a hot spring day, I found the site exactly where the book said it would be. Ann Price, a woman in her nineties, who lives today in the half-timbered house mentioned in the guidebook, happened to be in her yard that day, and she knew everything about Perry. Her grandparents had known him well. After he'd died, they'd even bought his home, demolishing it to make way for the house Ann lives in now. Regarding the fairy legends, she had little to say. Although her face lit up at the mention of Perry's name, when I asked her about the folklore—"I have an allergy to that nonsense," she said.

Before long, Ann invited me inside to show me an old Victorian fireplace, the only surviving feature of Perry's former home. As we made our way through the yard, she pointed out the former location of the World's Smallest Store, now a bed of flowers and grasses. Inside, she showed me photos of Perry framed on her bookshelves: in one, he's sitting cross-legged on the stoop of the World's Smallest Store; in another, he's standing next to his wife, Martha, looking suitably elfish, ears pointy, with a wandering eye; and in another, he's wearing a top hat and standing with a dog beside a gramophone. (Apparently, he used both dog and gramophone to entertain people during one of his get-rich schemes.)

James Perry Wanzer (also known as Perry Boney) and his wife, Martha, outside their home in the early twentieth century. *Photo courtesy of Ann Price.*

Thanks to Ann Price's uncle Julius Wilson, we have a vivid description of Perry's appearance that gives some serious "fairy changeling" vibes. I'll quote it here in full because it evokes the strangeness one must have felt when meeting him. It's perhaps this strangeness that accounts for his association with fairies, for even when the fae appear quite human, they possess an otherworldliness that gives them away, or so the legend goes.

"His narrow, sly, and dirty face," wrote Julius, "was always obscured by scraggly whiskers of several weeks' growth. His eyes were cocked and never looked at his interlocutor except sideways. His most striking anatomical feature was his terribly bowed legs, probably due to infantile rickets, which made him short and his arms seem long and which gave him a ludicrous rolling, pigeon-toed gait."

Such an unflinching description surely proves Perry Boney was real, right? Not quite.

In fact, *Boney* wasn't even Perry's real name. The authors who first wrote about him, mindful of the relatives who wished to protect the family name, used the name Boney to disguise his true identity. Nobody wanted to give an eccentric like Perry unfiltered publicity; it was too embarrassing. In 1855, he was born into an old Dutch family called Wanzer with roots going back to early 1700s Connecticut. The Wanzers had become comfortable in Sherman after many years of farming. They owned nice tablecloths, a luxury back then, and could afford to pay for help. Unfortunately, for Perry Boney (real name, James Perry Wanzer), his father, George, was a wild man prone to fits of rage. He had a reputation for sleeping with his much younger servants too. This included Phebe, who later gave birth to Perry.

Illegitimate, unwanted and with a father whose hollering scared even the neighbors, poor Perry never stood much of a chance in life. At twenty-five, he met Marthy Crowfoot, the woman he'd live with for the rest of his life. She became a rather scolding wife.

Poor Marthy must have suffered, though. Perry couldn't keep a job. He hated labor and was always coming up with doomed moneymaking schemes, whether turning the local schoolroom into a makeshift movie theater to sell tickets, taking to the road as a fairground photographer, making root beer in his wife's washtub or buying Fairfield County's first wind-up phonograph to put on "entertainments" that never covered the cost of the technology he'd bought.

Perry soon became known as a do-nothing and a layabout. His wife, Marthy, became a cleaner for Ann Price's grandparents, the distinguished Reverend Warren Hugh Wilson and his wife. Their daughter, artist Margaret

Wilson, later recalled hearing about the raucous nights at Perry and Marthy's shack beneath Coburn Mountain. Perry would dress in a "thirdhand clown costume" and Marthy would commandeer a puppet show. Such entertainments never drew anybody respectable, though they demonstrated Perry's showmanship. He was an actor at heart, said Margaret.

Considering everything we know about Perry's eccentricity, must we forever put to bed his association with the Good Folk? According to Ann Price, yes. Otherwise, we perpetuate inaccurate folklore. The truth of history is more interesting, she said.

One thing we can say for sure is that, by 1938, when Perry's story appeared in the Connecticut guidebook, he'd become inextricably associated with fairies. This was seventeen years after he died of heart or kidney failure in 1921. The guidebook's writers must have visited Sherman before they wrote about Perry, and perhaps while they were there, they heard the Wanzer children tell some tale about the fairies. For all we know, those children might really have believed he spoke with fairies, that he was one of Eve's unwashed children. Or perhaps the crafty Wanzer way was to joke that an embarrassing, illegitimate relative was actually a fairy changeling?

Perhaps we'll never know if Perry talked to fairies or if fairies inhabited the pools along Greenwoods Brook. Those who wish to investigate may do so. I did not see them anywhere but did experience the untouched beauty of the place. One thing we can't do is hold the fairies responsible for Perry's death; they didn't take him, and we know exactly where his body lies: in Sherman's Center Cemetery beside his wife's.

THE FAIRY VILLAGE IN THE WOODS

A time comes in the life of every youngster growing up in the town of Middlebury when he or she learns about the collection of tiny fairy houses lying neglected and abandoned in the woods outside of town. Some hear about the throne in the middle of the village. It kills anyone who sits on it within seven years. Others learn that a crumbling, human-sized house made of stone lies beside the village and that the man who lived there, driven to madness by elvish voices, built the tiny village for the fairies in the woods. The red-painted throne was said to have been erected for the most important of fairies: the King of Fairyland.

Those who seek out this tiny village may stay to drink beer, graffiti the crumbling wall, or sit on the throne for a laugh or a dare. After they leave, they may feel the atmosphere of the place has sunk into them, leaving them with a palpable dread. Or perhaps they feel nothing at all. Either way, those who visit may mention it in passing to a friend or relative, and hence a legend is sustained.

Two versions of the site's fairy story have circulated through the years. The first is that a man and a woman who lived in a stone house in the woods built the village on the woman's insistence. She wished to pacify the malicious elves who lived thereabouts. Their chattering voices instructed her to do so. The second is that an old man, living alone in the same house and driven to madness by the fairies, constructed the village for the little ones to live in. Ever since, dark spirits have lurked in the shadows of the tiny buildings and the old stone house. The lore's focal point appears to be the cursed and death-dealing throne, which only the foolhardy and disbelieving will sit on.

The site can be visited today via a winding, abandoned service road off Route 63 opposite Maggie Mcfly's restaurant. Sidestep a barrier, follow the road beyond the power lines and find the trail to the village on the left. On a visit in the spring of 2023, I must confess I made it only as far as the ruins of the house. I saw the "fairy tunnel" beside it (the function of which is now unknown) and one fairly intact fairy house. Seized with a feeling of unease, I couldn't bring myself to explore the rest, meaning I didn't see the legendary fairy throne—red and resplendent at the heart of the village—or the other tiny houses, which apparently have crumbled to almost nothing by now. Don't judge me, reader, but I took a photo and left.

What is it about this odd attraction that unsettles visitors so much? It cannot be anything to do with the real-life backstory that reporter Erik Ofgang uncovered in 2020. There's nothing disturbing about it. A man called William Lannen bought the site in 1924 to build a gas station. When a bypass route put an end to his business, he established a plant nursery. To attract more customers, he built a miniature village complete with doll-sized homes, winding asphalt roads, miniature cliffside properties, tiny steps and even electric lights. Eventually, for unknown reasons, he abandoned the idea and moved on. The attraction never opened, and there was nothing supernatural about it, but thanks to a plucky reporter, we know the truth.

The truth won't necessarily inure you to the site's unpleasantness, and even Ofgang, the reporter, admitted to a feeling of "unease" when visiting

Miniature house at the Little People's Village in Middlebury. Legend says it was built for the fairies. *Author's photo.*

the place. His head filled with stories he'd heard about the "otherworldly creatures that supposedly haunt the air here," and how those who stay too long "hear the fairies and go mad," he found the "haunting" site had spooked him.

Others who've shared their experiences also attest to the strangeness of the location. One man called Tom, commenting on a *Damned Connecticut* blogpost, claimed to have visited the site with his sister in 2009 and seen a "white cloud or mist" rising through the glass of his camera lens. Although he snapped a photo at just the right moment, the picture captured no mist. Others claim to have heard laughter coming from the trees in the vicinity, found their cameras had died despite being recently charged or felt a sensation like a ghost passing through their flesh.

Do these experiences confirm the power of suggestion, the hold such disturbing legends wield over us, or are they symptoms of being "pixie led"—that madness brought on by the presence of fairies? I wasn't willing to stick around to find out.

SUMMARY OF THE FAIRY CENSUS FOR CONNECTICUT

The three Connecticut stories offered in this chapter in no way exhaust the fairy experiences reported in the state. The Fairy Census of 2014–2017 fills us in on the types of phenomena people have experienced, which they believe were fairy encounters. The two census entries I offer here demonstrate that the fairy faith in Connecticut takes the form of belief (i.e., ideas about fairies) and experience (i.e., encounters with fairies).

The first fascinating entry suggests that, since at least the 1930s, four generations of Connecticut women have passed the fairy faith from generation to generation. The respondent in question explained to the census that her mother had found a diary belonging to her grandmother, a "second generation American of Scottish/English descent," in which she found entries dated to the 1930s when her grandmother must have been in her twenties. The now-deceased grandmother described seeing fairies "in her garden" and "along the edge of the woods." She claimed they were "human-like," with "wings like insects," and said they were "fluttering about and…tending to their own business." The respondent said she was now a firm believer in fairies and that her twelve-year-old daughter was too, suggesting the fairy faith, brought here from Scotland or England, had become firmly established, passed through three further generations of Americans.

Another Connecticut story from the census describes a young girl's intimate encounter with a fairy one afternoon when she was "playing in the woods." After climbing a "large glacial rock," she met an extremely "tall thin man" whom she "just knew" was a fairy. She described his face as "angular" and his fingers as "long and pointy," with six on each hand. She spoke with the man for a long time, but afterward, she couldn't remember what they'd spoken about. When she climbed down to go home, she saw that the man had disappeared. She also explained her philosophy of the fae, writing that fairies are "beings who vibrate at a different frequency and are in a parallel dimension."

2

MAINE

Maine is probably New England's most welcoming state for fairies. Visit any of the islands along the rugged coast and take a short walk into the piney woods; chances are you'll come across a tiny home at the base of a tree or a whole village of tiny houses, each constructed from natural materials like stones, twigs and cones and often complete with walkways, turrets and everything else that makes a good home. These are Maine's fairy houses, usually fragile, seasonal residences, which families with children like to make for the fairies as they wander the islands' trails in designated "fairy zones."

The tradition of building tiny homes for the fairies began on Monhegan Island, twelve nautical miles from the mainland, and quickly spread to Mackworth Island and many of the other islands dotted along the Atlantic coast. How the tradition began is a mystery. Some claim British and Irish settlers brought stories about fairies to the islanders, who quickly took to welcoming the fairies with makeshift homes. Others say schoolteachers traveling from the mainland to educate the islands' children in the early 1900s imported ideas about fairies that inspired the islanders to build homes for the Little People in the woods. Whether the homes were originally intended to house real fairies or were simply used to encourage children to connect with nature is unknown.

Maine's fairy houses may be a living testament to fairy folklore, but many would argue they represent a whimsical activity rather than an actual belief. Some people have invented stories about the houses, including one

Examples of fairy houses found at the Community Fairy Village on Mackworth Island, Maine. *Author's photos.*

particularly colorful tale in which the fairies built the homes after setting sail from western Ireland and arriving in Maine on the backs of silver eels and clumps of seaweed from the Sargasso Sea. However, these stories are clearly fictional, intended to entertain children. For those wishing to learn about bona fide fairy beliefs in Maine, the state has plenty of examples to offer the curious, in no small part due to the sheer variety of influences permeating the state's fairy folklore since the eighteenth century.

In Maine's early days, parts of the state belonged to the New France colony of Acadia, and in the nineteenth century, other French Canadians immigrated here, bringing French ideas about fairies with them. In this chapter, I provide a summary of French Canadian fairy stories collected throughout Maine in the 1960s by students of the University of Maine. These students' grandparents and other relatives cultivated many folkloric ideas about fairies, thereby preserving a record of ancestral fairy belief originating in France.

Before the French and English settled Maine, Native American tribes such as the Penobscot and Passamaquoddy cultivated incredibly detailed beliefs about fairies and fairylike beings, which they began to share with folklorists and anthropologists in the late nineteenth century. Three magical beings, among others, can be found in their stories: *alombegwinosis*, or dwarves, who lived under the surface of the Penobscot River; *mikummwessuk*, or Little People, who lived deep within the woods and sometimes collaborated with Passamaquoddy shamans; and *oonohgamesuk*, or water fairies, who lived in rivers and lakes and on the shore of Passamaquoddy Bay. Each magical being had a slightly different function or behavior for the Native American tribes, and here I try to tease out some of these differences.

I should note that the Wabanaki stories I recount in this chapter are largely historical in nature, concerning events from the nineteenth century through to the 1960s. In his book *Where the Lightning Strikes*, anthropologist Peter Nabokov, who spent three months on Indian Island as a guest of the Penobscot in the late 1970s, attests to the continued importance of the Little People to the Wabanaki people. One night during his stay, the Penobscot told him to stay in his room after twilight for "his own good." The next day, when visiting an elderly parishioner of St. Anne's Church, Nabokov learned that the Little People had emerged from the woods the night before, "covered in…twinkling lights." The anecdote offers a rare glimpse into the continued relationship between the Penobscot Nation and their magical neighbors.

Finally, I end the chapter with a summary of the Fairy Census's findings for Maine.

LUTINS AND FEUX FOLLETS

The farthest north one can travel in New England is Maine's fairy-haunted Aroostook County. Bordering Quebec to the west and north, and New Brunswick to the east, the county is far removed from New England's major population centers and has historically received the greatest French influence of the region. It was Acadian families—descendants of colonists from the French colony of Acadia—who settled the Aroostook region in the 1780s. In the centuries that followed, other French Canadians moved here to become lumberjacks and potato farmers. Today, around 15 percent of Aroostook County residents speak French at home, and many continue to celebrate their French heritage at a cultural festival held each year.

Given the influence of French culture on this most northerly of New England counties, it's no surprise that Aroostook's fairy lore has exhibited a rather French flavor through the years. The French elf or hobgoblin called a *lutin* is perhaps Aroostook's most famous fairy. Similar in appearance to a red-capped elf like the Norwegian *nisse* or Finnish *tonttu*, the lutin was generally considered to be a household or farm-dwelling spirit who entered people's homes or barns to bring mischief or luck, as the case may be. The lutin loved to ride horses and was forever stealing into farmers' barns to braid the animals' manes, forming stirrups, which he used to ride them through the night.

According to the U.S. National Park Service, lutin stories were particularly prevalent in Aroostook County's St. John Valley, home to Maine's Acadian community. One survey respondent told a National Park Service researcher that "lutins…live in caves and come out only at night." The respondent explained that the beings are so tiny that nothing can prevent them from entering people's homes, for they pass through apertures as small as a keyhole.

Despite the commonly held belief that lutins are found most prevalently among the Acadians of Aroostook County, the majority of lutin stories collected by folklorists in Maine appear to have been drawn from farther south and derive from the memories of later French Canadian immigrants. These immigrants tended to share stories they'd heard from elderly people in their ancestral lands, whether Quebec or New Brunswick, and they rarely spoke about lutins actually living in Maine.

A handful of well-known stories about lutins derive from the recollections of a French Canadian American man called Emile Levesque who lived outside Augusta, Maine, in 1968. Levesque learned his stories from his father, Ferdinand, and it appears the events (which Levesque described as "just stories" and not real) took place in Trois-Pistoles, Quebec.

Above: Horse with "fairy locks" or a plaited mane by Peter Schenk the Younger (1752). *Public domain.*

Left: Modern depiction of a lutin, a gnome or household spirit found in French fairy legends. License: https://creativecommons.org/licenses/by-sa/3.0/legalcode. *Image by Godo.*

Levesque's most famous story, immortalized in Michael Parent's book *Of Kings and Fools*, concerned a farmer who believed lutins had taken up residence in his barn. At night, the lutins would harness the farmer's horse and ride off in his hay wagon. Where they went, the farmer couldn't say, but he decided one night to hide in the wagon and find out. The story, as related by Parent, continues as follows:

> *Around midnight, the barn doors opened. In no time at all, a "little man," no more than three feet tall, harnessed the horse to the wagon, and off they went....The man's house was not far from the sea. Suddenly, the wagon rode onto the water....Then, he heard, "Whoa!" and the wagon stopped. The* lutin *put the reins down (and) jumped off the wagon—Ploop!— onto the water, lit a small lantern, and walked away from the wagon.*

Watching from the wagon, the farmer saw he was floating on the sea and that fifty or more twinkling lights were bobbing above the water, each light representing a lutin's lantern. The lutins were apparently enjoying some kind of assembly while walking on the surface of the sea. (The lutins' association with the sea in this story recalls, perhaps coincidentally, the etymological roots of the word *lutin*, which can be traced back to a type of sea monster.)

Another story told by Levesque involved a little boy who was extremely afraid of lutins. He believed they dwelt in his family's barn. When the boy's father asked him to water the horses in the barn, the boy never wanted to go, and the father would have to force him. One night, the boy came running back from the barn and almost broke the door down trying to get inside the house. He said he'd seen a lutin with a head the size of a "walnut" and eyes as big as his fist. (The point of the story seems to be the humorous effect of the child's description, in which the lutin's eyes are far bigger than its own head, proving, perhaps, that the child had made the story up.)

Levesque's final story concerned a farmer whose land simply crawled with lutins. So many mischievous elves had taken up residence on his property that they eventually broke into his house and destroyed everything, upstairs and down. Consequently, the farmer decided to move his family and possessions to another plot of land. But just as the family were riding away in their wagon, a lutin emerged from a bouquet of flowers among their possessions. The farmer was dismayed to find he'd brought the "accursed" lutins with him!

Another Augusta resident and student at the University of Maine, Richard Beaudoin, collected lutin stories from the largely French-speaking or bilingual Augusta community in 1968. Beaudoin claimed to have grown up hearing his father mention lutins, but neither he nor his father had ever seen one. In fact, his father's stories were already old in 1968, and Beaudoin said they rarely concerned lutins actually living in Augusta or the surrounding area. Rather, lutins had been "objects of fear," he said, to the old men his father had known in Quebec. The father blamed these men's fear of lutins on their superstitious nature.

The secondhand, Canada-based nature of many Maine lutin stories can be seen in one Augusta man's claim that, as a boy growing up in Quebec, he'd worked with men who told stories about lutins who tied "almost impossible" knots in the logging chains at lumber camps. These knots, the man claimed, "were almost impossible to tie because both ends of the chain were either tied to the horses or the sleigh."

Beaudoin concluded his collection of stories by stating that nobody he knew in the Augusta community had firsthand experience of lutins, as most of the information concerning them derived from memories of people's childhoods in Quebec. To Beaudoin and his young peers, lutins were hardly recognizable beings, and no young people he interviewed could tell him any stories about them.

Acadian residents of Aroostook County, on the other hand, definitely told stories about Maine-dwelling lutins. One man, Joseph Normand Grinnell, who hosts a glossary of Acadian French words on his website, claimed that between 2004 and 2012 he met various Acadian residents of the St. John Valley whose grandparents believed in lutins. "One person," he wrote, "told me that a now-deceased elderly lady asked him to go into her garage to chase away *les lutins*. He went in there, came out, and told her that he chased them all away. Another elderly person told me about his late father-in-law. The father-in-law once went into a barn and claimed that he saw *les lutins* doing something to the mane of his horse."

Even if many of Maine's stories about lutins take place across the Canadian border, it's clear these mischievous elves have made a home away from home for themselves in New England's most northern state. Christopher Packard suggested as much in his book *Mythical Creatures of Maine*, where he explained that his great-great-grandfather Burton Marlborough Packard learned in 1894 he had a lutin on his property; a local Frenchman told Packard he was "lucky" to have the lutin because it was sure to "look after the place."

THE MYSTERIOUS FRENCH FAIRY known as a *feu follet*, "fire sprite," is best described as a type of will-o'-the-wisp or jack-o'-lantern. It resembled a green, blue or bright white flame that sometimes floated above a marsh or swamp but could also be found in towns. Known to the Acadians of Aroostook County, these fairy flames were thought to differ from their European counterparts, the will-o'-the-wisps, in one crucial aspect. As Christopher Packard has pointed out, the will-o'-the-wisp tended to lead people into dangerous marshes or swamps, whereas the feu follet was far more likely to "chase people." Instead of following these magical lights, Acadians were forced to run from them.

In 1965, University of Maine student Geraldine Cormier, who lived in Presque Isle, learned from her mother that the feu follet was "just a little tongue of fire," usually seen at night. Despite her mother's unimpressive description, Cormier knew these fairies were no joke. For the feu follet was hardly a friendly fairy, and if you called one by a "vile name," the sprite would "get angry" and "really fly after you," sending you running.

Based on Cormier's description of the fairy, it's likely her mother was describing events that took place in Canada, for she said the feu follet was often seen coming up "from the sea shore." By this, she meant a location in New Brunswick.

Other manifestations of the feu follet have certainly occurred in Maine, however, including one woman's story about a fairy fire that followed a man through the town of Presque Isle as he walked to a dance one evening. The woman explained that "some people thought dancing was evil in those days and the feu follet was really chasing René." The man only managed to shake off the sprite by running to a neighbor's house and falling through the door. Interestingly, it seems the fire may have been attracted to the man because he was about to engage in the possibly "evil" activity of dancing. Just as fairies are repulsed sometimes by holy objects, perhaps they're sometimes drawn to things considered less than holy.

THE MAGICAL DWARVES OF THE PENOBSCOT RIVER

Alombegwinosis. The word is long and, for English speakers, difficult to pronounce. But in the Algonquian language of the Penobscot people—a tribal nation occupying Indian Island in Central Maine—the word means "underwater man-dwarf." It refers to a fairylike being, about three feet tall, that lived in deep pools in the Penobscot River, close to where the Penobscot made their homes. Frank Speck, the anthropologist we met in the chapter on Connecticut, who interviewed Fidelia Fielding, first publicized this piece of Penobscot folklore in the 1930s when he described a "shy man-like dwarfish being" who possessed "considerable power." Speck learned the story while sitting around a campfire with Penobscot men "enjoying an after-dinner smoke."

According to Penobscot lore, these dwarves lived alone or in warrior bands, always residing underwater—in rivers like the Penobscot or in lakes. They had the ability to alter their size magically, whether adopting a great stature or making themselves so small they could hide inside a leaf. Three feet tall in their normal state, the dwarves went about naked with their straight black hair uncombed and falling below the waist. They were known to eat from cooking vessels in which they'd place a kernel of corn. When they removed the kernel from the vessel, it would magically provide more than enough to eat.

Although these dwarves tended to shy away from human contact, they sometimes allowed themselves to be seen, but this was never a welcome sight. For the appearance of an alombegwinosis was a premonition of drowning to the one who saw him. According to Speck, the Penobscot believed that anyone who saw one would drown within a year. One of these dwarves was known to live in a deep pool in the river opposite Indian Island in the town of Milford. One night, a Penobscot man who'd camped near the pool woke to see the dwarf, which quickly disappeared under the ice. "Within a year," Speck wrote, "the man himself was drowned by falling through a hole in the ice."

Another dwarf was thought to live forty miles north of Old Town near Lincoln Island in the Penobscot River. The dwarf's abode was a deep pool near a "dense growth of pines and hemlocks." Legend says a man, determined to catch the dwarf, once buried himself in some sand near the pool. He thought the dwarf would bring him luck or bestow on him magical powers. After a few attempts, the man managed to catch the dwarf, which begged to be released. He even offered up his sister as a bride if the man would only let him go. The man agreed and received the dwarf's bow and arrow as guarantee that the dwarf would return. Soon enough, the dwarf appeared at the man's home and handed over his sister in exchange for the bow and arrow. The sister had brought a cooking vessel, a tiny pot capable of receiving only one kernel of corn. When she cooked the kernel, to the man's astonishment, the vessel overflowed, producing far more than they could eat.

View of the Penobscot River and Indian Island in Maine, where dwarves were believed to live in deep pools. *Author's photo*.

While researching these stories, I traveled to Central Maine to explore the environs of the Penobscot River. After checking in at the Milford Motel, I sat on the balcony overlooking the river, in the middle of which stood Indian Island, home of the Penobscot Nation. I watched people canoeing below the balcony, oblivious to the dwarves who, according to legend, lurked there long ago. In olden times, no canoe was completely safe, for a dwarf could easily upset one and pull the paddler down.

Not all Penobscot stories about the alombegwinosis are scary though. In fact, the most detailed story we have about one of these watery dwarves is rather funny. According to Speck, Penobscot storytellers had a great sense of humor. Almost all their stories were funny or had an undercurrent of humor, and this is clearly a feature of the following tale about the futility of vain wishes.

In the story, a storm-harassed dwarf found himself washed up on a lakeshore, almost dead, when a Penobscot man rescued him and took him home. The man's family was very poor, and the wife hated the sight of the dwarf, having a mind to kill him. The dwarf said that if the woman let him live, he'd bestow upon the family three wishes. The man and woman let the dwarf go and began to think about how they might use their wishes. The woman went straight to a local trading post where the Penobscot bought their household items. Seeing a broom, she immediately wished to have it. When the woman returned home, her husband was angry because she'd wasted a wish on such a mundane item. In his irritation, he wished it was up his wife's anus, and immediately, it happened, almost killing her. The broom could only be removed when the woman's son wished it was out of her. The three wishes all used up, the family remained as poor as they were before they'd had them.

SHAMANIC FAMILIARS AND WATER FAIRIES

The folklore of the Passamaquoddy people, whose home stretches from eastern Maine to New Brunswick, Canada, is full of references to magical beings. The most important of these is undoubtedly Glooskap, a divine lord and hero whom the Great Spirit created and gave power to shape the Passamaquoddy people. He taught the Passamaquoddy skills associated with civilization such as how to grow corn and hunt. He's also credited with creating or shaping a whole host of magical creatures as well as humans and the animals of the forest. After accomplishing many labors and going on many adventures on behalf of the Passamaquoddy people, he withdrew from the land the Passamaquoddy call Dawnland (for its proximity to the rising sun) and set up home on a distant island, where he promised that anyone who found him would be rewarded with magical wishes.

When Glooskap first appeared in the land, long before he created human beings out of the bark of an ash tree, he made two types of fairy beings. Later, when Glooskap made the Passamaquoddy, these magical beings continued to live in close proximity to humans, although usually hidden from them. The first of these beings was called *mikummwess*. Translated as "Little People," the mikummwessuk (plural) had a long and varied relationship with the Passamaquoddy Tribe, first attested in the 1880s and continuing into the present.

The mikummwessuk were originally depicted as little men who lived in the woods and had magical powers. Although they were generally encountered in pairs or in groups, one mikummwess, in particular, became very well-known to the tribes of the Northeast. This was Glooskap's companion, a friendly being called Apistanewj. The name translates as "Marten" in English, for he could transform himself into a marten, a creature related to the weasel. Marten was Glooskap's adopted younger brother and accompanied him on many adventures through the lands of the Wabanaki tribes, sometimes borrowing his magic belt to acquire superhuman strength. Besides being an animal shapeshifter, Marten was one of the mikummwessuk and spent a great deal of time in the Little People's homes among the rocks and rivers near Passamaquoddy homes. In this role, he was called Mikummwess and usually took the form of a youth, but he could also transform himself into a baby, small boy or young man.

Fortunately, a few images of mikummwessuk created in the late nineteenth century have survived, which helps us imagine what they may have looked like. The first is a sketch by the folklorist Charles Leland. The second is an etching in a birchbark container by the Passamaquoddy artist and governor Tomah Joseph. Leland's sketch, based on one of Joseph's etchings, features an elven figure with two pointy ears wearing a cap. Leland claimed the being always wore a red cap like a "Norse goblin," an apparent reference to the Norwegian *nisse*. History has revealed that Leland may have embellished or altered aspects of Passamaquoddy culture to reflect his own interests. This means that Tomah Joseph's etchings probably represent a more authentic depiction of the Little People.

Charles Leland's copy of a Tomah Joseph etching of a mikummwess or Little Person. *Public domain*.

One of Joseph's images, found on a birchbark container in a private collection, shows the diminutive mikummwess holding a long-stemmed pipe and sitting on a tree stump beside a river. The image suggests the Passamaquoddy saw the mikummwessuk as friendly, nature-dwelling beings. (A similar image of a mikummwess can be seen on the side of a birchbark canoe that the Passamaquoddy gifted to Franklin Delano Roosevelt before he became president. Joseph was a friend of Roosevelt and even taught him how to paddle his canoe. The canoe bearing the fairy image is now on display at the Roosevelt Campobello Island Museum in New Brunswick.)

Although shy, the mikummwessuk were not totally uninterested in humans. They sometimes gave their powers to men, thereby turning the recipient into a shaman or transforming him into a fairy. The earliest story to feature such a transformation appears in Mi'kmaq legends. It's said there that after Glooskap left the world to dwell on a far-off island away from the Native American tribes, a young man wished to become one of the mikummwessuk. He'd heard that the divine lord would fulfill the wishes of anyone who set out to find him and succeeded. The man went on a long pilgrimage in search of Glooskap and finally found him on his lonely island. Receiving the young man, Glooskap guided him through a mystical initiation. First he covered him with filth and washed him in a river. Then he combed his hair, changed his clothes and put a magical "hair string" around his neck. He taught the man how to sing enchanting songs and gave him a magical pipe that granted him power over all living things. This ceremony transformed the man into one of the mikummwessuk and gave him, in Leland's words, "all the power of the elfin-world."

The notion of elven transformation in this legendary account continued into the twentieth century when Passamaquoddy tribe members reported real-life stories of magical transformations. They believed the mikummwessuk could act as shamanic familiars, in other words, beings that initiated Passamaquoddy men into the spirit world and bestowed upon them magical powers. In 1899, an old Passamaquoddy man called Newell S. Francis, who grew up at the tribe's Pleasant Point home in Coastal Maine, described meeting a shaman when he was fifteen years old, whom he called a mikummwess, a name the Passamaquoddy used to designate someone in possession of a mikummwess companion or familiar. Like the legendary account of the man who became a mikummwess, this shaman, according to Francis, possessed all the powers of the elven world. Proof that a man was in cahoots with a mikummwess was his ability to walk into the ground up to his ankles. This suggests that the powers of the mikummwessuk, as in other Native American stories about

Tomah Joseph's depiction of a mikummwess on the side of a birchbark wall pocket. *Charles and Barbara Adams' private collection.*

Little People, included the ability to move underground and pass through tiny spaces. This way of walking was called "walking like a shaman."

The relationship between Passamaquoddy shamans and Little People continued into the 1960s and 1970s, when tribe members who lived at Indian Township and Pleasant Point, the two Passamaquoddy reservations in Maine, described a shaman as someone who'd partnered with a mikummwess. Long ago, they said, the mikummwessuk appeared to the Passamaquoddy to foretell major events such as the election of a new governor. They did this by performing Passamaquoddy dances and ceremonies in the woods. However, at some point they no longer appeared to the tribe and remained invisible to anyone except a shaman who had the power to see them.

After the Passamaquoddy Tribe's conversion to Christianity, partnership with a mikummwess became increasingly controversial, and in the 1960s, one teenager described such partnership as "selling one's soul." The teenager's cousin had apparently sold hers to one but had later "returned to the church." Nevertheless, belief in the mikummwessuk continued in some capacity, with one woman describing the Little People as extremely friendly beings who spoke so fast and in such a high-pitched voice that it was impossible to understand them. If you met one, she said, he'd never let you leave because he'd want to talk to you so much.

As the influence of Christianity took hold, the mikummwessuk became increasingly frightening, suggesting a process of demonization in the eyes of the community. Rather than being described as little men, they became hairy and often had horns. More and more, their presence became associated with tribe members who practiced witchcraft. When they weren't bargaining for people's souls, they'd peer into windows and throw rocks, apparently embodying antisocial behaviors. If tribe members witnessed such behaviors—even when it was teenagers carrying them out—they'd blame the mikummwessuk. This allowed them to cast judgment on the behavior without implicating anyone in particular. The anthropologist Willard Walker called this a function of social control, a way for the tribe to condemn behaviors without ruffling anyone's feathers. Fulfilling a similar role, the Little People sometimes punished people who violated the sanctity of the local church, chasing, for instance, one man who tried to steal the sacramental wine.

AT THE DAWN OF time, when Glooskap made the Little People or mikummwessuk, he also gave life to the oonohgamesuk, a word usually translated as "water fairies." We'll hear more about these beings in the chapter on New Hampshire, where they lived near the Saco River in the White Mountains. They also lived in Vermont under a related name, as we'll see in that chapter. As for Maine, the water fairies made the great mountain of Katahdin their home, as well as the Penobscot River and its tributary, the Kenduskeag. The remoteness and inaccessibility of these homelands inspired folklorist Charles Leland to call the water fairies "wondrous dwellers in the lonely woods."

In the nineteenth century, the tribes in northern New England knew the oonohgamesuk under various names according to the Algonquian dialect they spoke. The Penobscot of Central Maine called them *wenagameswook* and said they had extremely thin faces "like the blade of a hatchet," meaning they could be seen only in profile. They described the fairies as having large "aquiline noses" that took up most of their faces and mouths shaped like the letter *A*, the point ending beneath the nose. Rather than offering individuals magical powers like the mikummwessuk, the wenagameswook were thought to appear to tribe members to warn them of future events such as deaths or Mohawk raids.

Mount Katahdin, where the water fairies lived, according to Charles Leland. *Library of Congress.*

One of the most famous stories we have about the water fairies concerns two Penobscot hunters returning in a canoe from their winter hunting ground. The hunters spied ahead of them a canoe containing what appeared to be two small boys. As much as the Penobscot men paddled, they couldn't catch up with the boys' canoe: the boys always remained at the same distance ahead. Eventually, the boys stopped paddling, and it was then the hunters realized they were actually two little men. "Nowut Kemaganek Meguyik," said one of the little men, using the Penobscot language, which translates as, "There are Mohawks at Nowut Kemaganek." The Mohawks were enemies of the Penobscot, and the water fairies had decided to warn the men about a future raid. When the hunters arrived home, the tribe's elders believed what they reported right away because the water fairies were known to foretell terrible events, whether by appearing to the tribe in person or carving petroglyphs (writings in rock) along the river.

Although the Penobscot believed the water fairies lived in deep pools in rivers and danced on the banks like "jolly elves," an old man called Sauk Ketch who lived at Old Town claimed in 1833 that the tribe no longer saw the fairies in their usual haunts along the Penobscot River. All they saw were the products of their labor: artifacts made in clay, often representing humans and animals, which the water fairies created in the night and left beside rivers. The Penobscot believed the figures brought them luck. (We'll hear more about these clay artifacts in the chapter on Vermont.)

The water fairies showed themselves to the Penobscot again in 1833 when the aforementioned tribe member, Sauk Ketch, went hunting with three other Penobscot men and came upon the fairies' footprints in a sand bed in the Kenduskeag Stream. Ketch's tall tale, which I recount here, suggests the Penobscot believed the water fairies were ancestrally related to the Wabanaki tribes of the Northeast, as we'll see. It should be noted, however, that the story, while "allegedly true…doesn't match the current normative culture's standards for reality" (in Peter Muise's words). In other words, it's extremely fantastical.

After coming upon the water fairies' footprints, Ketch and his three friends followed the prints until they discovered a tiny village made of clay, which they knew the water fairies must have made. Not wishing to remain too long in the vicinity of these magical beings, they continued upstream and before long saw a crowd of little men running back and forth on a sand bed. The Penobscot men watched them for a while from their canoe—they were "wrestling, jumping, and playing"—until a sentinel got wind of them and cried out, "The Devil!" Instantly, he ran for the water, shouting, "Next Monday past noon one notch," which the Penobscot took to mean one o'clock. Thereupon, all the water fairies dived into the river and disappeared.

Sauk Ketch, believing the sentinel's shout meant the fairies would return at one o'clock next Monday, hatched a plan to conceal himself in the sand and try to catch one when the time arrived. Sauk returned with his friends at the appropriate time, covered himself in sand and waited until he heard the fairies' footsteps above him. At that moment, he leaped up and managed to catch two of them in his hands. They struggled to escape, covered "their faces with the sand" and begged Sauk not to look at them. Nevertheless, he caught a glimpse of their "beautiful hair," narrow eyes and extremely long chins, which reached almost to their chests.

Finally, the water fairies said that if Sauk let them go, they'd show him the island where they lived in a nearby lake. The Penobscot men freed the fairies and followed them to an island, where they saw "crowds of little people hurrying and running on the shore." In the midst of them was a large man, lying on his back and snoring, whom the fairies identified as their king. He wore a green jacket with a blue and red lining, "close-fitting leggings" and "black shining moccasins with a silver clasp."

The fairies told the men they were one of twelve tribes dispersed over the earth, a king ruling over each. They believed the Penobscot descended from a related but "lost" tribe that had claimed the "earth" as its "mother," the fairies having claimed the water. They said the twelve tribes' kings liked to eat Penobscot children who fell into swamps and rivers and drowned. Eventually, they told the Penobscot to leave and began hoisting ladders to tend to their sleeping king. They combed his gray curls and carried buckets of water to wash his face. In silence, the men left and never saw the fairies again.

The relationship between the water fairies and the Wabanaki tribes didn't end with Sauk Ketch's encounter in 1833. In the 1960s, the Passamaquoddy Tribe used a modern but related word, *winokomehsuwok*, to refer to the water fairies that lived near the tribe's Pleasant Point reservation. At this point in history, different members of the tribe described the water fairies in different ways. Some said they were little green men like leprechauns. Others said they didn't exist and that "unruly children" were sometimes mistaken for them. Still others insisted they did exist and that they were similar to the Passamaquoddy except they were little and had thin faces. One girl said she thought they lived in the rocks along the coast "on the other side of the highway," always near water. Like the mikummwessuk, they had the ability to foretell future events, and if, for instance, a wedding was about to take place, they'd sing a wedding song. Elders would warn children that if they strayed too close to the highway or Passamaquoddy Bay's shoreline, the water fairies would take them, and they'd never be seen again. The anthropologist Willard Walker identified this as an example of magical beings embodying social harms, thereby protecting children from danger. Whereas the fairies had once warned the community about potential danger, they now represented the danger itself.

SUMMARY OF THE FAIRY CENSUS FOR MAINE

The Fairy Census of 2014–2017 offers two stories from Maine. The first, which occurred in the 1980s, concerns a teenage girl who was standing in her yard with her mother and her aunt. They had just begun to admire the flowers when a "rather large" bumblebee landed on one of the flowers. Immediately, all three women noticed the bee had a "tiny red pail" hanging from its front legs. The pail appeared to be metal because it was "shiny." Within a minute or two, the bumblebee was gone. After the encounter, the girl's mother said the creature must have been "from the fairy realm, because in our world it was highly unlikely an oversized bumblebee would be collecting nectar in a shiny red pail the size of a thimble."

In the second story, which took place in the 2010s, a woman in her forties was walking along a woodland path when she saw movement about twenty yards from the trail. The woman left the trail and found a "too pale being washing her wings in the river." The woman was very tall, had lemon-yellow wings and smelled strongly of cinnamon. Although the walker went back to the spot a few times, she never saw the strange being again, but she could still smell the cinnamon. "I'm not certain she was fae," the woman wrote, but "ghosts don't smell and angels don't need to bathe." The woman believed that fairies were "parallel universe beings."

A few things can be said about these fairy beings. Both appear to inhabit a world distinct from ours but overlapping with it. The first being came "from the fairy realm," according to the respondent's mother; the second was from a "parallel universe." Both beings appeared in our world and interacted with objects existing inside it, such as a flower and a river. They also performed actions typical of beings who exist in our world, including gathering sustenance and bathing. The fact that they were physical beings can be seen in their use of a tool (the pail) and their noticeable scent. It appears the beings occupied a mystical world overlapping ours and neither seemed particularly interested in their human observers. In this way, it seems to me that both stories feature quite traditional depictions of fairies, rather unlike the spiritualized fairies or beings of light we'll encounter elsewhere in the census.

3

MASSACHUSETTS

From pixies to pukwudgies to Little People dwelling underground, Massachusetts is home to a bewildering array of fairy beings. In particular, the Wampanoag Tribe who live at Mashpee on Cape Cod and Aquinnah on the island of Martha's Vineyard have a long history of telling Little People stories. These stories represent Massachusetts's most deeply rooted and widespread fairy traditions, probably originating in precolonial times. When the English settlers arrived in Massachusetts in 1620 and built their homes on Wampanoag land, many of the region's Native inhabitants may have professed Little People beliefs. The same cannot be said, however, for the settlers themselves. European fairy traditions had little opportunity to become established in Massachusetts because the early settlers didn't usually believe in fairies. This isn't to say that *no* European fairy lore took root here: as we'll see, the town of Marblehead on the state's North Shore welcomed many immigrant believers in fairies from South West England. Their stories and traditions flourished well into the late nineteenth century.

Marblehead—which I like to call the Pixie Capital of the United States—is a picturesque seventeenth-century fishing town located on a hilly peninsula sixteen miles north of Boston. Settled by hardworking and hard-drinking fishermen who weren't particularly invested in Puritan ideals, the town proved a more fertile place for fairy lore than perhaps anywhere else in New England. As someone who comes from England's southwest region myself, I couldn't help feeling a certain affection for these

Set of stone steps used by Marblehead's eighteenth-century fishermen. License: https://creativecommons.org/licenses/by-sa/4.0/legalcode. *Melissa M. Stewart*.

settlers as I researched their fascinating stories. Raucous and anarchic, they loved to tell a good story, and even the proximity of Salem's litigious Puritans couldn't stop them. Here I provide a summary of Marblehead's fairy beliefs as they existed in the town in the late nineteenth century.

The rest of the chapter mostly focuses on stories associated with the Wampanoag Tribe. No treatment of Massachusetts fairy lore would be complete without a reference to the Wampanoag's infamous *pukwudgie*, a fairy being responsible for much murder and mayhem if modern accounts are to be believed. Even the oldest pukwudgie folklore characterizes these Little People as causing harm to human beings while lurking in out-of-the-way corners of the state's natural landscapes. Originally, this meant the marshes around Popponesset Bay on Cape Cod, but over the years, pukwudgie stories have widened to include ominous territory such as the Freetown State Forest, five thousand acres of woodland with a reputation for dark happenings and ghostly hauntings. Nowadays, people are far more likely to associate pukwudgies with Freetown than with the Cape, and this has had the unfortunate side effect of obscuring interesting Wampanoag stories.

Other stories retold here with definite or possible Wampanoag origins include the tale of the Little People of Aquinnah on Martha's Vineyard and the story of the Little Man of Chappaquiddick. Both narratives suggest that long before the Wampanoag told stories about pukwudgies, the Native American inhabitants of eastern Massachusetts had other traditions of Little People, which they probably taught to the Mohegans. As mentioned in the chapter on Connecticut, the Wampanoag shared much of their folklore with the Mohegan Tribe. This included stories about the friendly giant Maushop and his wife Ol' Squant or Granny Squannit.

Although no section in this chapter is entirely devoted to Granny Squannit, the Wampanoag who lived at Mashpee told many stories about her, describing her as possessing fairylike qualities. To the Wampanoag, she appeared to be a little woman with a "three-inch footprint," about the size of a rabbit's. The folklorist William Simmons described her as the Mashpee Wampanoag's most ubiquitous folkloric figure, much older than the pukwudgies and probably having origins in a Native goddess of women and children. The Wampanoag left offerings to Squannit outside her cave on Sandy Neck Beach or on tree stumps in woodlands. While often considered a benevolent figure who taught the Wampanoag useful skills such as healing with herbs, she also had a dark side and was invoked to warn children against straying or being naughty. "Granny Squannit will take you," the elders would say. One of her most mysterious features were her eyes, which the Wampanoag depicted as either square or cat-like; others said she possessed only one eye in the middle of her forehead. Most of the time she covered her face with her long hair, and like the Mohegans' makiawisug, she could point at someone and disappear.

Perhaps because Massachusetts is by far the most populous state in New England, modern fairy beliefs are well-represented in the Fairy Census of 2014–17. Eight responses, more than any other state, are recorded, and many of these stories (mostly told by women) concern fairies that resemble glowing blue and white lights. Most of these fairies are nonthreatening, appearing in the guise of benevolent nature beings, although one respondent did share experiences involving beings with clear malicious intent. Another respondent saw a fairy that looked to have an "evil nature," although this was speculation based on the fairy's appearance. The conclusion to be drawn from all this is that the fairy faith is alive and well among a small section of Massachusetts residents and that modern-day fairies are generally seen as small, beautiful, benevolent and light-emitting beings.

THE FAIRIES AND PIXIES OF MARBLEHEAD

When I say that the town of Marblehead on Massachusetts's North Shore is unlike other coastal Massachusetts towns, I'm not simply referring to the fact that it's teeming with fairies and pixies (which it is). Isolated from the state's highway system on a remote peninsula, the town has always boasted a most unorthodox history. Think of it as the black sheep of colonial New England. Whereas Puritans founded the surrounding settlements of Salem, Peabody and Danvers to be pure and godly communities, Marblehead's beginnings were more down-to-earth. According to historians Priscilla Sawyer Lord and Virginia Clegg Gamage, "irreligious settlers" and "adventurous fishermen" founded the town to escape the harsh dictates of Puritanism while making a living catching fish. In about 1629, these humble but industrious early settlers headed southeast to a peninsula where the Naumkeag Tribe lived. They coexisted peacefully with the tribe while establishing the sleepy fishing village we know today.

Over the next few hundred years, Marblehead saw an influx of fairy-acquainted immigrants from Scotland and the fishing regions of South West England: Cornwall, Devon, Dorset and Somerset. According to the historian Samuel Roads, immigration from England's South West accounted for what he called Marblehead's "idiomatic peculiarities," a fact we'll discuss in more detail later in the context of the distinctly Marblehead word *pixilated* and its interesting connection to the fae. Besides their linguistic idiosyncrasies, the townspeople also had an approach to life that was noticeably cheerier than that of their Puritan neighbors. The first reference to the name *Marblehead* in the colonial records (at that time, the village was under Salem's jurisdiction) came in 1633, when a man called John Bennett was fined for being drunk on the "Sabbath day."

Such raucous beginnings characterized the spirit of Marblehead for many years, for the Cornish and South West English who lived there rarely belonged to a church and didn't establish one in the town until 1684, although they did build a meetinghouse to host religious services on a hill overlooking the harbor. Unlike their Puritan neighbors, they imported from England unorthodox ideas about fairies and pixies, too. If it's true to say that where the Puritans went, the fairies didn't follow, it might also be true to say that where the Cornish and South West English went, the fae usually flourished. Based on English fairy lore, early Marblehead's lack of a church might even have encouraged the fairies to come, for there's nothing the Good Folk hate more, apparently, than the tolling of a church bell.

The first record of Marblehead's thriving belief in fairy legends came in 1851, when the son of Supreme Court justice and Marblehead native Joseph Story described the town as home to a "compendium of all varieties of legends" that "credulous" immigrants from "all over the globe" had brought to Massachusetts. Some of these immigrants, from Devon, brought with them a belief in pixies; others, from Scotland, brought a belief in bogles (a type of goblin or bogeyman); while others, from the north of England, brought a belief in jack-o'-lanterns (light-bearing fairies similar to will-o'-the-wisps). Justice Story recalled the town's superstitious fishermen warning him to run home at twilight so the bogles wouldn't catch him. In fact, belief in "hobgoblins," among other supernatural beings, was almost "universal" in the town, claimed Story.

A few decades later, in 1894, the outside world got wind of the sheer extent of fairy lore in modern Marblehead when a woman called Sarah Bridge Farmer put to writing what she'd heard as a child from the town's elderly residents. She described what has since been recognized as Marblehead's most notable contribution to fairy lore: a clear distinction between good fairies and bad pixies.

According to Farmer, the fairies of Marblehead looked kindly upon the town's residents and never did anything to harm them. The elders told her that children needn't fear the fairies because they were "universally sweet-natured." They were known to live in "underground palaces built of gold and silver, ornamented with pearls and precious stones."

These elaborate underground homes clearly derive from English fairy lore, in which they're a common motif. However, in England, this aspect of fairyland was more complicated than it at first appeared. Often, when humans visited a fairy abode, the grandeur of the place would impress them, but the appearance was nothing but enchantment and "glamor." The enchantment would inevitably wear off, and the visitor would find himself in a cave with only dirt and leaves for decoration.

Following Marblehead's winding streets to the tip of the peninsula, one can see why the town's residents might have located the fairies in underground palaces: the town boasts many hills, both steep and gentle, covered in moss and clover. Fairies have long been associated with mounds—sometimes called *hollow hills*—and one Marblehead hill, in particular, has a very fairylike atmosphere: the location of the old burying ground, where the colonial-era dead are buried above the town. (It seems to me there's something a bit eerie about a town where members of the living go about their activities somewhere below the dead.)

Other Marblehead beliefs about the good-natured fairies included the fact that they visited the human world only to revel on moonlit nights, that they left "fairy rings" of moss or fungi where they danced and that they drank from red lichens shaped like wine glasses. When the dawn came, they'd hurry back underground or fall asleep among the flowers, where children would look for them, believing that if they caught one, it would bring them luck.

Marblehead's pixies, on the other hand, were "malicious" creatures that, like the fairies, were "tiny" but brown colored. They loved to lead people astray at night, causing them to wander for hours not recognizing familiar sights. As in parts of Rhode Island, one way to protect oneself against pixie enchantment was to "turn one's clothes." This meant turning out the pockets of one's coat or turning an entire garment inside out. The practice confounded the pixies and prevented them from exercising their malicious enchantment. One Marblehead resident, an elderly, well-educated woman, claimed the pixies caused her to wander for "an hour or more unable to find her home." Eventually, she realized the "little brown people" had cast their enchantment over her, and she "turned her cloak," breaking the spell. The word used for this pixie-induced bewilderment was *pixilated*.

Marblehead's residents were famous for their unique way of speaking. This included broad pronunciation of vowels and strange idioms unknown

Pixies playing on animal bones from J. Jacobs's *More English Fairy Tales* (1894). *Public domain.*

to other New Englanders. They always dropped the letter *h* at the beginning of words, clipped their words short and used a dialect reminiscent, according to historian Samuel Roads, of a "cockney Englishman's." Few Marblehead expressions have received as much attention, however, as the word *pixilated*, which appears, in America at least, to be unique to the town.

First attested in the mid-nineteenth century but probably used much earlier, the word may have originated in the term *pixie led* or (in the academic Simon Young's opinion) in a Somerset term, *pixie laden*. Like Marblehead's pixie enchantment, pixie led referred to a state of being lost or confused at night. It could also refer to madness more generally or a state of being "beside oneself." The meaning of the word *pixilated* in Marblehead is therefore consistent with its South West English origins, where pixies also led people astray, especially when someone was returning home drunk from an inn or local booze-up. Records of the word being used in the town lend credibility to Sarah Bridge Farmer's descriptions of Marbleheaders' thriving fairy beliefs.

THE PUKWUDGIES OF POPPONESSET BAY

Pukwudgies are perhaps Massachusetts' most famous magical being, helped, in part, by J.K. Rowling's inclusion of them in her wizarding world (for the record, she gave the name Pukwudgie to a scholastic house at the American Ilvermorny School of Witchcraft and Wizardry). Unfortunately, as the stories in this chapter make clear, misinformation about pukwudgie folklore is rife throughout popular culture. Appearing first in Wampanoag folklore as warlike Little People with magical abilities, they've morphed in recent years into creatures or cryptids, very different to the beings they once were.

One claim about pukwudgies popularized in books and websites on Massachusetts folklore is that they're troll-like beings with porcupine quills and that they live today in the Freetown State Forest. There they enjoy terrorizing hikers and have been known to push people off the 130-foot-high Assonet Ledge. As a result, pukwudgies are now closely associated with Freetown, as well as the whole "Bridgewater Triangle," a supposed hotspot of supernatural activity in southeastern Massachusetts. Meanwhile, stories about these supposedly forest-dwelling beings have largely eclipsed the authentic Wampanoag folklore in which they originally appeared.

The modern troll-like version of the pukwudgie found its clearest expression in 2017 when the Freetown Police Department posted a warning sign in the forest featuring a picture of a troll with quills, the words "pukwudgie crossing" printed underneath. The truth is, the oldest Wampanoag stories about pukwudgies don't contain references to the Freetown State Forest, and nowhere does the folklore describe them as troll-like beings with porcupine quills.

The earliest references to pukwudgies in Massachusetts can be found in the stories that two Wampanoag Tribe members, Red Shell and Wild Horse, related to folklorist Elizabeth Reynard in the early 1930s. In their stories, the pukwudgies were little men who lived in the salt marshes around Popponesset Bay on Cape Cod, where they organized themselves into seven bands of warriors each with its own chief. These pukwudgies had a warlike nature, a fact that became apparent from the violent pranks they liked to play on the Wampanoag. They also liked to tease the benevolent giant Maushop, who was thought to reside near Falmouth on Cape Cod and whom we met in the chapter on Connecticut.

The pukwudgies in the Wampanoag stories were two feet tall, built their homes in "high grasses or bulrushes" and possessed powerful magic, which they used for evil ends. Sometimes they taught mysterious swamp lights, called will-o'-the-wisps, to lead Wampanoag men and women into the marshes, where they'd become trapped in quicksand or drown. Sometimes they appeared in the form of wild animals, such as bears or mountain lions, to terrify Wampanoag women and children. And sometimes they shot Wampanoag tribe members with poisoned arrows or pushed them off cliffs. Just when it seemed a Wampanoag hunter might catch one, the pukwudgie would magically disappear.

It's clear from these stories that pukwudgies—like the Little People in Passamaquoddy and Penobscot folklore—embodied the Wampanoag Tribe's immediate and long-standing dangers, whether the threat of wild animals or the risk involved in traversing local landscapes. We saw in the chapter on Maine that stories about Little People and water fairies often functioned to protect a tribe from danger, especially when told to children. Similarly, the pukwudgie acted as a reminder to the Wampanoag of everything they ought to avoid if they wished to survive in the land, including swamps, cliffs and wild animals. *Avoid* here seems to be the right word, because the pukwudgies, as we'll see, could never be defeated.

According to Red Shell and Wild Horse's stories, even the friendly giant Maushop failed to stop their evil doings. A heroic figure in Wampanoag

Marshes around Popponesset Bay where the pukwudgies made their homes. *Author's photo.*

folklore, Maushop taught the Native Americans many skills, including the crafting of weapons and tools. Slow to anger but possessing a fierce temper once he got going, Maushop was particularly protective of the Wampanoag, and one day he decided to solve the pukwudgie problem forever.

First, he looked for the pukwudgies in the Popponesset marshes, hoping to sweep them away with a stroke of his giant hand. Then he peered into the bullrushes, looking for their tiny homes. But the pukwudgies could remain extremely still, and as soon as he approached, they'd simply disappear. Irritated by his lack of success, Maushop sent his five giant sons to look for them. The giants lay in the piney woods and waited for the pukwudgies to appear. But the Little People could move so stealthily through the tall grasses, the giants never stood a chance: the pukwudgies threw sand into the giants' eyes, blinding them immediately. Then, retreating a short distance, they shot the giants with poison darts, causing them to die a slow and painful death. Not long after, the pukwudgies even managed to drive Maushop from the land. (The folklorist William Simmons argued that telling such stories gave the Wampanoag a way to express criticism of the European settlers who'd stolen their land, the pukwudgies standing in for white people.)

Red Shell and Wild Horse's stories about pukwudgies are fascinating on many levels. But to understand the pukwudgie's true nature, we have to consider older sources. The word *pukwudgie* isn't original to Wampanoag folklore and isn't actually a Wampanoag word. In fact, it comes from the Algonquian language of the Ojibwe people, who lived in the Great Lakes region of North America. The Wampanoag storytellers—who told the first stories about Massachusetts's pukwudgies in the 1930s—apparently adopted the word to emphasize the tribe's cultural association with other Native American tribes and restore what they saw as the tribes' spiritual commonalities. These cultural insertions were later reported as authentic folklore—for example, in Jean Fritz's popular children's book, *The Good Giants and the Bad Pukwudgies*.

The folklorist Henry Schoolcraft traced the origin of the pukwudgies to a boy called Wa-Dais-Ais-Imid who appears in an ancient Ojibwe legend. The legend suggests that at some primordial point in time when everyone living on the earth had died, a young brother and sister who'd survived the near extinction set up home together beside a lake in the Great Lakes region. When the boy and girl grew up, the girl suspended a "small shell" around her brother's neck, thereby naming him Wa-Dais-Ais-Imid, "he of the small shell." Despite the years that followed, the boy never grew, and even after he reached adulthood, he remained the size of a small child. Eventually, he chose to become a "wild man of the mountains," a term Schoolcraft transcribed (in the Ojibwe language) as *puckwudjininee*. This little man said he would take up residence in the "mountains and rocks," where the "streams are clear" and the "air pure" and where his "kindred" would "ever delight to dwell." The implication is that every pukwudgie who ever lived descended from this man.

The pukwudgies appeared again in Ojibwe folklore as antagonists of a hero called Kwasind, a man whose feats of supernatural strength, including single-handedly clearing pine trees from a path and fighting the giant King of Beavers, excited the pukwudgies to envy. They feared he'd take away all their work and drive them into the lakes, where they'd drown. Knowing that Kwasind's strength resided in the crown of his head and only pinecones could kill him, the pukwudgies gathered on a clifftop above a river where Kwasind was known to canoe. When he passed directly below the cliff, they threw their cones at Kwasind's head and killed him. The Ojibwe hero sank beneath the water and drowned. In Ojibwe folklore, Kwasind's story functions as a warning against boasting, for Kwasind incited the pukwudgies' envy when he boasted about his strength.

The pukwudgies attack Kwasind in M.L. Kirk's illustration to *The Story of Hiawatha: Adapted From Longfellow* (1910). *Public domain.*

The story of Kwasind and the pukwudgies later appeared in Henry Wadsworth Longfellow's *The Song of Hiawatha*, which is probably where Red Shell and Wild Horse got the idea to use the word as a name for the Little People of Wampanoag tradition. That the pukwudgies were originally seen as Little People (the word literally meaning "wild man of the mountains") and not troll-like beings with quills is clear from early illustrations, such as Maria Louise Kirk's 1910 illustrations for *The Song of Hiawatha*, which depict them as miniature humans. It isn't clear how or why the troll-like pukwudgie appeared, but it may have had something to do with the 1982 publication of *The Good Giants and the Bad Pukwudgies*. There the pukwudgies are depicted as tiny, gray-skinned trolls with large black manes. It seems the manes were later turned into quills.

Since the magical pukwudgies of Native American folklore have been transformed into twenty-first-century cryptids, a handful of people claim to have seen them in the Freetown State Forest. One report, found in Christopher Balzano's book *Dark Woods*, comes from a woman who was walking her dog in the forest when she saw a pukwudgie "with pale gray skin and hair on his arms and the top of his head." Eerily, the pukwudgie followed the woman home and watched her through her bedroom window at night. Another report, found in the same book, described the pukwudgie as a hairy little man with glowing red eyes. Clearly, twentieth-century pukwudgies are far more monstrous than the miniature beings of Wampanoag lore; the latter, despite practicing hostile magic, more closely resembled humans, even organizing themselves into tribes with separate chiefs, rather like the Wampanoag.

My final word on pukwudgies, ancient and modern: If you visit Popponesset Bay and find yourself in the vicinity of the marshes, especially where the tall bulrushes grow, watch out for the horse flies. Not only will they land on you and bite you, but there's also the possibility they're pukwudgies in disguise. One of the Little People's favorite activities was to transform themselves into flies to bite Wampanoag men and women. As for the Freetown State Forest, I walked alone (reluctantly) to Assonet Ledge in the heart of the forest to take photos. Although I heard a few rattlesnakes shaking their tails and encountered a couple of cyclists, I didn't see any troll-like pukwudgies, and nobody tried to push me off the ledge. However, the forest was eerily deserted, and I could see why stories about its malicious denizens might flourish. If you visit, be careful where you tread: if not a rattlesnake, you might disturb a pukwudgie.

View from the Assonet Ledge in the Freetown State Forest, where legend suggests pukwudgies push people to their doom. *Author's photo.*

THE LITTLE MAN OF CHAPPAQUIDDICK ISLAND

A two-minute ferry ride from Martha's Vineyard will take you to the tiny island of Chappaquiddick, where the Wampanoag Tribe likely told stories about Little People to the English immigrants who arrived on Cape Cod. Many tribe members once lived on the island, a small piece of land 527 feet to the east of its larger neighbor. After the Europeans brought diseases to North America, the number of Wampanoag on the islands dwindled, and today about five hundred tribe members live on the whole of Martha's Vineyard year-round. We know the Wampanoag located the Little People around Popponesset Bay on the Cape and in Aquinnah on Martha's Vineyard. However, another story comes to us from the nineteenth century that might represent a vestigial trace of earlier Wampanoag stories focused on Chappaquiddick Island: the story of the Little Man of Chappaquiddick. Although the story derives from early twentieth-century descendants of the English who'd taken up residence on the island, the folklorist William Simmons argued that the English probably learned the story from the Wampanoag, who perhaps told it to them while sitting around their campfires.

In 1918, the folklorist Ben Clough published the Little Man's story in the *American Journal of Folklore*. He described how those who live on the island sometimes encountered a little man while walking through the island's moors. All they could say about him was that he looked very strange— "queer-looking," in fact—and that as soon as they saw him, he would point into the distance. When the viewer looked in the direction he was pointing, the man would disappear.

The only complete story we have about the Little Man of Chappaquiddick involves a visitor from Martha's Vineyard who encountered the Little Man in a farmer's field. As he always did, the Little Man pointed and disappeared. When the visitor asked the farmer who the Little Man was, the farmer said that both he and his father had seen the man but neither knew anything about him. "You've seen him!" said the farmer. "Now maybe folks won't say there's no such thing."

William Simmons pointed out the similarities between the Little Man's behavior and the behavior of the makiawisug of Mohegan Hill (see the chapter on Connecticut): both miniature beings point and then disappear. Whereas the makiawisug tend to point at the person they wish to hide from, the Little Man points in some other direction and disappears only when the beholder looks away. Based on these similarities and the fact that the phenomenon occurred on ancestral Wampanoag land, Simmons believed the story had Wampanoag origins and was transferred to the English at some later date.

One caveat about the reliability of this story is that Clough, who first recorded it, said the visitor from Martha's Vineyard was known to be a "lover of practical jokes." Although the story he related has generally been taken as evidence for the wider occurrence of Little Man encounters on the island, this appears to be an assumption based on only one piece of evidence. Skeptics might well question whether the farmer who claimed to have seen the Little Man was simply responding in kind to the man's practical joke. Perhaps we'll never know if the Little Man was real or simply an amusing prank.

THE LITTLE PEOPLE OF AQUINNAH, MARTHA'S VINEYARD

The town of Aquinnah on the remote western tip of Martha's Vineyard (or Noepe, as it's called in the Wampanoag language) has been the center of Wampanoag life on that island for several hundred years and is home to a number of magical beings from Wampanoag folklore, including the Little People. Once named Gay Head after the variegated colors of the cliffs along the seashore, it reverted to its original name, meaning "land under the hill," in 1997. The Wampanoag Tribe's stories about Little People survived well into the twentieth century in Aquinnah, although folklorist William Simmons claimed that, by 1983, nobody remembered them. The worker I met at the Wampanoag Museum in Aquinnah was unfamiliar with Little People stories but knew a lot about Maushop the giant. Nevertheless, the stories were attested in 1925 when tribe member Rachel Ryan shared a particularly vivid story about an underground fairy realm with the folklorist Gladys Tantaquidgeon.

The events occurred in a place called Duncan's Ridge where the Wampanoag men and women went to pick huckleberries. In those days, Gay Head derived much revenue from berries, and each year, the townspeople selected a day when all the residents went out to pick them. On the day the story's events took place, a beautiful Wampanoag woman, known locally as a doctor or medicine woman, went to pick the berries with her neighbors and stayed behind when they went up on the hill to feast. When evening came, the community realized the woman hadn't returned, and although

The clay cliffs at Aquinnah, Martha's Vineyard, close to where the Little People lived underground. *Author's photo.*

they searched for her everywhere, they could find only her basket, which they hung on the branch of a tree. They hoped she'd return and retrieve it, for she was greatly respected in the town for her healing abilities. Every year, when they picked the huckleberries on the appointed day, they'd look with sadness at the hanging basket. It degraded more and more each year until only the "bail" remained.

Many years later, when the townspeople were at Duncan's Ridge again picking berries, they saw a woman climbing the hill toward them. To the Wampanoag, the woman looked unusual because her hair was "kinky," whereas their hair was straight. When she arrived at the ridge, she said she belonged to the tribe and that she'd gone missing from that spot years before. The tribe's chief denied it, saying the Wampanoag have straight hair but she had kinky. She must be a "stranger," he said. Undeterred, the woman affirmed her tribal membership and told the following story.

On that fateful berry-picking day, when she rested from her work on a rock, a small man with black skin approached her. He said his king was in great pain and asked if she'd come with him to take a thorn out of his side. She followed him down a long flight of stairs until they were deep underground.

They came to a "beautiful realm" where the people, like the man, were little and had "kinky" hair. The woman extracted the thorn from the king's side and nursed him back to health. This impressed the Little People so much they gave her gifts. However, when she expressed her desire to go home, they wouldn't let her leave. The king's son had fallen in love with her and wanted her to be his queen. She refused. It was forbidden to marry a member of his race, she said, and this enraged him so much he grabbed her by the hair and dragged her around until her hair became "kinky." Finally, he allowed her to depart but only after taking away the gifts the people had given her. It took her a long time to climb the underground steps, but she finally made it home.

Before mentioning the chief's response to the woman's story, I ought to point out that today the tale is generally considered to be a racist story. Not only does it express anxiety about Black people's arrival in Martha's Vineyard and their intermixing with the Wampanoag, it also describes a social hierarchy in which the Wampanoag come out on top. The chief's response was as follows: "This foretells the coming of another people whose hair will be tight, and woe unto you when they appear." He said the coming race would intermix with the Wampanoag, and the woman would be "the ancestor of many kinky-haired Indians." He then commanded her to be cast out of the tribe.

If Rachel Ryan's story about the "little black man" with "kinky hair" suggests racism existed toward African Americans among the Wampanoag Tribe in the 1920s, this seems not to have been the case in the 1850s. In that decade, Wampanoag Tribe members were instrumental in helping two men, Randall Burton and Edgar Jones, avoid arrest after escaping from slavery. Two women of the tribe hid Burton in a swamp near Aquinnah. As for Jones, tribe member Beulah Salisbury Vanderhoop dressed him in women's clothing and hid him in her home. They both eventually escaped to Canada.

SUMMARY OF THE FAIRY CENSUS
FOR MASSACHUSETTS

The Fairy Census of 2014–2017 includes eight responses from people living in Massachusetts. Six of these describe experiences of fairies taking the form of small, bright lights that either moved intentionally or appeared in the respondent's peripheral vision. It should be noted that most of the respondents described the lights as bright white or blue: these appear to be the two colors most often associated with modern-day fairies. All the respondents who saw these lights were female, and every experience took place in a garden or a woodland. The experiences are as follows:

One respondent described a childhood fairy experience in which she saw a flash of light and felt an "emotional presence." She believed the presence was "from earth" (i.e., it was not angelic) but not her "plane of existence."

Another woman, walking with family and friends through the woods toward a lake, saw "orbs of light the size of a fist," which she felt sure were fairies. They "floated a couple of feet off the ground and moved in a soft bob" before moving "into the woods and out of sight." The respondent's mother, sisters and friends also saw the lights.

A pagan minister officiating over a wedding ceremony with a bride who believed in fairies saw a "shimmering in the upper branches of a pine tree." She believed the shimmering came from fairies who wished to take part in the ceremony.

A woman in her forties, alone in her yard, asked the fairies if they'd appear in a photo for her. When she snapped a picture, she saw in the camera what she described as a "fairy light" or "light blue blur." This woman's fairy beliefs seemed similar to Dora Kunz's (see the introduction), because she described fairies as "mostly beneficent but with their caring directed toward nature."

A woman walking in a wildlife reservation saw a flash of "cobalt blue with bits of red" between the trees; when she went to investigate, there was nothing there.

A woman walking in a Massachusetts forest watched as a ray of sunlight hit the ground in front of her and turned a "very intense neon blue." A white light emerged from the ray's center and began to move up and down and side to side. The woman took a picture in which she claimed to see a blue ray with a white figure inside it.

These experiences are fairly similar, involving flashes of color or slow-moving light but rarely suggesting a humanoid form. The fairies described seem intimately associated with nature, appearing among trees and in woods. The following story differs greatly and is the only response provided by a man.

The respondent, a man in his twenties, heard strange animal noises around his home in the week leading up to the encounter. His mother and fiancé also heard them but, after investigating, found nothing. Late one evening, he heard a knock at his bedroom window, as if a bat had flown into it. When he got up to see what it was, he spied through the glass what appeared to be "a small person" about "two to five inches in length," "very shriveled," almost like a "mummy," with "dragonfly-like wings." His fiancé also saw it momentarily.

As the being was dark in color and looked "mummified," it occurred to the man it had an "evil nature," but he didn't report any feelings of fear. The being's humanoid appearance, dark color and overall ugliness differ markedly from the light-emitting or beautiful fairies that other respondents reported. A similar phenomenon of both ugly and beautiful fairies can be seen in the Fairy Census for New Hampshire, as we'll see.

The last respondent is also the one who shared her experiences most exhaustively. The fairies she claimed to have encountered can be divided into four different types: tall, elven beings; a female figure who sang to her in a language she couldn't understand and who nursed her head while she slept; male fairies whom she didn't see but who talked about her and, disturbingly, groped her breast before leaving; and lastly, a "bright, pale, luminescent figure," about six or seven inches tall, with a bald head, antennae, pointy ears and large, dark, slanted eyes. The woman's encounters are astonishingly varied. If the reader wishes to learn more about them, I recommend looking at the Fairy Census.

4

NEW HAMPSHIRE

Traveling through the forests of New Hampshire in the shadow of the White Mountains, one can see why so many of the Granite State's residents have told stories about fairies over the last few hundred years: in summer, the state's landscape is a veritable fairyland of mountains, waterfalls and forests.

A rich tradition of fairy stories has taken root in the state, beginning with the Abenaki, who first traversed these lands, continuing with the stories of Scots Irish and English immigrants in the eighteenth and nineteenth centuries, and surviving even into the modern era when many people might tell you the fairy faith is dead. If fairies are real—and I, for one, have never seen one—there's no doubt New Hampshire's hills and forests provide abundant hiding places for them. If the fairy visionary Dora Kunz is to be believed, many types of fairy are indeed concealed here. And even if you don't believe in fairies, it cannot be denied that the European immigrants who established New Hampshire's villages and towns created the perfect environment in which stories about them could emerge.

I began my research into New Hampshire's fairies beside the sparkling waters of Derry's Beaver Lake, supposed home of a "fairy queen" called Tsienneto (pronounced Shaw-nee-to), who, in 1697, intervened dramatically in the life of an Englishwoman called Hannah Duston. The story, I discovered, is one example of the types of stories told by the descendants of Scots Irish immigrants who founded the New Hampshire village of Derry in the eighteenth century.

The term *Scots Irish* refers to Scottish immigrants who settled in Ireland's Ulster province in the seventeenth and early eighteenth centuries before moving across the ocean to build their homes in New England. The Scots Irish brought their fairy lore to North America even earlier than many of the other immigrants we've met in this book, and traces of this lore survived into the twentieth century. As we'll see, their stories combine Scottish (and perhaps Irish) fairy lore with tales of American folk heroes, creating a fascinating blend of Old World and New World ideas.

A further example of European fairy lore emerging in New Hampshire is the story of a young boy's encounter with a tiny fairy in the village of Campton in the 1830s. Told by the boy's mother to her grandchild many years later, and then passed on to a twentieth-century folklorist, the story suggests that elements of English fairy lore may have come to New Hampshire as early as the seventeenth century and that subsequent generations kept them alive before putting them down in writing.

Abenaki fairy stories occupy an important place in this chapter. Native American Little People traditions are found throughout the Algonquian-speaking Northeast, so it's no wonder the Abenaki, New Hampshire's dominant tribe, told stories about fairylike beings. Their descriptions of water fairies in the White Mountains provide us with two stories here, the first focusing on Diana's Baths, a natural beauty spot in North Conway, and the second on a waterfall called Waternomee Falls in the woods near Warren.

Besides these folkloric stories, fairy visionary Dora Kunz has populated New Hampshire's forests with a bewildering array of magical beings. While staying at a friend's cabin in the New Hampshire woods, she encountered various types of fairy, each as colorful as her imagination was powerful. She saw "tiny fellows about a foot tall, of a rich golden brown," with faces "like little monkeys," who spend their time tending to the "ferns and mosses." She also saw "small brown and gold" gnomes, "deep blue fairies about eighteen inches tall" and water fairies who lived in the brooks—"tiny, slender things which look like translucent pale blue water."

As well as these diminutive fairies, Kunz described other fairy beings "of human size and form," almost with "the standing of angels," who were "perfectly colored in yellow and green." Standing over them all was a "brooding" angel resembling "a clean-shaven youth with fine dark hair and a powerful aquiline face, his body enveloped in a lovely apple green."

Kunz was not particularly concerned with the Granite State's native folklore, and her observations rarely parallel descriptions of fairies that New Hampshire residents saw in the nineteenth and twentieth centuries. They do, however, share some characteristics with stories reported in the Fairy Census, which I share at the end of this chapter. The discrepancy between Kunz's fairies and the other fairies found in New Hampshire is perhaps most apparent in the strange 1956 story of a man's encounter with a "green fairy" in the woods near Derry, which I also share here.

THE FAIRY QUEEN OF BEAVER LAKE

One of colonial New England's most shocking and gruesome tales is the story of the Englishwoman Hannah Duston and her Abenaki captors. In the late winter of 1697, while Hannah was held captive in an Abenaki camp located at the confluence of the Merrimack and Contoocook Rivers, she took a hatchet in the middle of the night, slaughtered four sleeping Abenaki adults and six Abenaki children (aided in the deed by a fourteen-year-old English boy) and made her escape. Whether Hannah's actions represented a desperate attempt to reclaim her lost freedom or an act of revenge for the events leading up to her captivity, we'll probably never know.

Hannah certainly had reasons for doing what she did, although the lengths she went to have caused many people to question her integrity. The Abenaki had not only raided her hometown of Haverhill, Massachusetts, and reduced her home to cinders, but also murdered her newborn daughter. Finally, they'd taken her, along with two others, up the Merrimack River toward Canada, where they hoped to sell their captives to the French (who'd ransom them back to the English).

The details of the story are controversial and contested, not least because they're based on an account found only in the writings of Cotton Mather, who interviewed Hannah at length. They're also inconsistent with what we know about Abenaki treatment of captives. We do know, however, that Hannah committed the murders and fled to safety in Massachusetts. The Abenaki scalps she took with her, which she planned to exchange for a reward, were the proof.

What does all this have to do with fairies, you might ask? The answer lies in the gradual folkloric embellishments and vivid imaginations of Scots Irish storytellers who lived in the village of Derry in southern New Hampshire. Over the course of the next two centuries, they transformed the narrative of Hannah's escape into a fairy story fit for Hans Christian Andersen or the Brothers Grimm.

Hannah Duston's escape. Relief by Calvin H. Weeks on the Hannah Duston Monument in Haverhill. *Public domain photo by Daderot.*

The mythology of Hannah Duston initially got off to a rocky start. By the nineteenth century, New England's residents had more or less forgotten all about her. It was only in 1821, when a volume of northeastern folklore drew attention to her story, that New Englanders began to rediscover what she did. Thanks to her audacious actions, she became a folk hero, a symbol of American resilience and superiority over the Native Americans. As for her association with Beaver Lake's fairy queen, the story appears to have developed in the following way.

First, the descendants of Derry's Scots Irish immigrants became increasingly interested in Hannah's story. In their retelling of the tale, they began to associate the story's events with their own geographical location, especially a large pond called Beaver Lake, which lies a few miles outside the town. They claimed that Hannah's Abenaki captors, following their Haverhill raid, must have passed through the Derry region on their way to the Merrimack River. The first night's encampment may even have been pitched, they said, on the shores of Beaver Lake. Of course, Derry didn't exist when Hannah and the Abenaki were said to have passed through, the

Beaver Lake in Derry, where, according to legend, the Fairy Queen Tsienneto met Hannah Duston and pledged to rescue her. *Author's photo.*

area being wilderness with no trace of Abenaki settlement, and there's no evidence they were ever there. However, for the Scots Irish of Derry, the feelings evoked in a story's telling always trumped historical facts.

Having located the captive Hannah on Beaver Lake's shores, Derry's residents then began to circulate an unusual tale suggesting that a "fairy queen" lived in the lake and that Hannah's escape had been achieved through the fairy queen's supernatural aid. This particular tale was preserved in the early twentieth century when a woman of Scots Irish heritage shared what her ancestors had reportedly told her. Known locally as Tsienneto, a name the Scots Irish took to be an Abenaki word, this fairy queen—who quickly became Neto—was fond of helping people in distress. She'd even been present on that fateful day when the Abenaki, with Hannah Duston as their captive, set up camp. When Neto saw Hannah languishing on the shores of her beautiful lake, she took pity on the Englishwoman, rose up out of the water and promised to help her escape.

The story goes that Neto followed the Abenaki party all the way up the Merrimack River. After arriving at Sugar Ball Island, she cast a spell over the Abenaki, putting them into a deep sleep. This gave Hannah time to grab the hatchet, dispatch her captors and escape. In reality, it's likely Hannah killed the Abenaki after adding a soporific to their food.

The Scots Irish of Derry were known for their fairy stories, and Tsienneto the Fairy Queen might well have been a genuine figure of their folklore, her story dated, perhaps, to the late nineteenth century or earlier. Descended from Scottish Presbyterians who'd settled for a time in Northern Ireland, the Scots Irish had carried their fairy traditions across the sea, first from their native Scotland and then from Northern Ireland. After arriving in New Hampshire, they continued their folklore-weaving ways and set about telling stories about American folk heroes like Hannah, embellishing them with fairy magic. Their treatment of Revolutionary War hero and Scots Irish icon John Stark—which I recount here—in many ways parallels the Tsienneto and Hannah Duston narrative.

John Stark was born to Scots Irish parents in Londonderry, New Hampshire, in 1728. He would grow up to become a New England hero, known for various feats including enduring Abenaki captivity, "running the gauntlet" in an Abenaki settlement (i.e., running between two lines of men who beat him with sticks) and distinguishing himself in the Revolutionary War for his involvement in campaigns such as the Battle of Bunker Hill. The stories of Stark's daring so entranced Derry's Scots Irish citizens, they no longer felt content to portray him as a mere mortal and decided

Statue of John Stark in Bennington, Vermont. Legend suggests the fairies protected him from British bullets. *Public domain photo by Hunter Kahn.*

to give his story a supernatural sheen, just as they had with the story of Hannah Duston.

Fairies, they said, must have protected Stark from British bullets. This is what made him such a successful soldier. For the Scots Irish, any action of sufficient bravery and might, especially one that conferred the immortality of fame, could be attributed to fairy aid, and in this they shared the storytelling impulses of the Greeks, who so often attributed divine favor to their heroes.

If the Scots Irish propensity for fairy embellishments explains the story of Tsienneto, where did the rather exotic name come from?

Late nineteenth-century writers suggested the name meant "sleeping in beauty" in the Algonquian language. However, there's no real evidence to suggest it's an Abenaki word. The Derry Museum of History offers the rather disenchanting explanation that authorities in Derry in the nineteenth century invented the word as a name for Beaver Lake. They wanted to give the pond a more poetic, Algonquian-sounding name in the hope it would draw tourists to the town in summer. The first person to tell a story about the Fairy Queen Tsienneto must have taken the pond's contrived new name and given it to the fairy, whose abode it was.

The earliest reference I've found to Beaver Lake as Tsienneto Lake is from 1856 in a book describing New Hampshire's churches. Before this, every reference is to Beaver Pond.

A later reference to another fairy inhabitant of Beaver Lake appeared in a locally published pamphlet from 1907 called *Tsienneto: A Legend of Beaver Lake*. The writer, R.N. Richardson, enamored of the lake's beauty, described falling asleep on the shore and seeing a "little old gray-visaged wood-nymph" in a dream. At first, the nymph acted shy, hiding herself in a purple-and-green-striped flower called colloquially a Jack-in-the-pulpit. However, succumbing eventually to Richardson's gentle probing, she agreed to tell him the legend of the lake.

The story the nymph told Richardson had nothing to do with a fairy called Tsienneto but concerned an Abenaki hunter and magician, himself called Tsienneto, who came to the region to set up a home on the "Isle of Great Enchantment," which, according to the story, lay in the middle of the lake.

The local Pawtucket Tribe didn't take kindly to Tsienneto entering their territory. One day, they ambushed him and brought him before their chief. In his anger, Tsienneto prophesied that white people would soon come and steal the tribe's land. "A peculiar people," he said, "with pale-hued faces, shall come from beyond the water. They will dwell unmolested in the places thus desolated." When the Pawtucket requested a sign to prove the prophecy was accurate, Tsienneto took a huge boulder and threw it across the lake, where it split open the largest pine on the opposite shore. This, of course, terrified the Pawtucket men.

Richardson ended his tale by accusing the wood nymph of inventing the legend. The only response his accusation received was the sound of the nymph's laughter as it blended with the bubbling of the brook. She'd apparently played a trick on him to test his gullibility.

FAIRIES OF THE WHITE MOUNTAINS

The White Mountains' lush green vistas suggest the perfect breeding ground for fairies. The Abenaki people who lived here told many fairy stories set among the mountains' brooks and hills. These stories often possessed a similar flavor to those found among Maine's Penobscot and Passamoquoddy. Like those tribes, the Abenaki associated magical beings with brooks and waterfalls, and their stories described the Little People as living in rocky pools in the mountains, similar to the alombegwinosis (dwarves) we met earlier in this book.

As we learned in the chapter on Maine, two special regions in New England can be identified as the home of the water fairies (oonahgemessuk in the Algonquian language). The first is the great mountain of Katahdin in Central Maine, which the folklorist Charles Leland described as "haunted and enchanted ground, abounding in fairies and other marvelous beings." The second region is the intervale or low-lying tract of land beside the Saco River in New Hampshire's White Mountains, especially the pools and waterfalls known today as Diana's Baths. These lie near North Conway.

These two locations are not the only places where the water fairies lived. Vermont's Abenaki and Maine's Penobscot also referred to water fairies using cognate words such as *manogemassak* (in Vermont) and *winokomehsuwok* (at Pleasant Point in Maine). Folklorists have translated these names variously as "water goblins" and "elves." The Penobscot also called them rock fairies because they were said to live in rock pools along the Penobscot River.

The New Hampshire home of the water fairies, Diana's Baths, received its English name in the mid-nineteenth century when a woman called Miss Hubbard, vacationing in North Conway, decided the series of ledges and waterfalls hidden in the woods reminded her of a landscape where the goddess Diana and her nymphs might bathe. Charles Leland was particularly scornful of this choice of name, calling it "ridiculously rococo" and evidence of the "absolute antipathy" Americans felt toward Algonquian names. Before their distinctly European rebranding, the falls were known by names such as *oonahgemessuk weegeet* (home of the water fairies) and *oonahgemessuk k'tubbee* (spring of the water fairies) because of their association with the Little People.

The folklore of the northern New England tribes, which an old Passamaquoddy woman called Mali Sipsis shared via interpreters in the 1880s, describes the oonahgemessuk as ancient, primordial beings whom Glooskap, a divine person or benevolent deity appearing in Algonquian

Waterfalls and pools of Diana's Baths, which the Abenaki called the home of the water fairies. *Author's photo.*

creation stories, formed before he made humans and animals. Glooskap was said to have lived among the tribes of northern New England from the earliest days, and according to at least one story, he not only made the animals of the forest but also created human beings and taught them skills such as hunting and tobacco cultivation. From the earliest days of their existence, the oonahgemessuk resembled little men and were said to dwell in rocks. This is perhaps why they gathered at the site of Diana's Baths, which to this day offers the perfect rocky pools in which fairies might thrive.

Few stories about Diana's Baths' water fairies have survived. However, one tradition, preserved in the book *Place Names of the White Mountains*, suggests they were hostile to the Sokoki band who lived near the Saco River. The fairies would gather on the waterfalls' rippling stone surfaces and torment the Sokokis with darts, attempting to drive them away from the territory. In response, the Sokokis prayed to a mountain god (or to Glooskap, according to one version of the story) who called a flood to sweep the fairies away. Since then, visitors have been able to visit the falls in peace and bathe in the fairies' former pools. This is something I highly recommend, if only for their exquisite natural beauty.

Traveling west to the town of Warren deep in the White Mountains National Forest, one finds another location long associated with water fairies: Waternomee Falls. One of the many waterfalls found throughout the White Mountains, the falls can be reached via a valley through which the Clifford Brook flows until it reaches a staircase of mossy ledges. According to folklorist Charles Skinner, the fairies liked to dance and sing in the moonlight on the ledges, which to us would be dangerously slippery.

Legend suggests the fairies were the children of local tribe members who'd been stolen "from their wigwams" and given "fairy bread" to eat, whereupon they instantly turned into Little People. Unlike the water fairies of Diana's Baths, and despite their proclivity for child abduction, the fairies of Waternomee Falls were apparently "innocent and joyous people." Reclusiveness appears to have been their rule of life, for they always lived in unfrequented locations, and when human civilization encroached on their territory, they retreated further into the woods. As Charles Skinner pointed out, they once lived in the woodlands close to human towns, but they retreated into the wilderness around Waternomee Falls after "churchmen and cruel rangers" drove them away. Although it's unclear where Skinner got his information, he apparently received it from Native American sources.

The notion of "fairy bread" has strong parallels in British and Irish fairy lore. In those traditions, people who visit locations where fairies are feasting must avoid eating their food at all costs. This is because a single bite can result in the human becoming one of the fae or being trapped in the fairy world. Sometimes fairies trick humans into eating their food as a way of detaining them in fairyland. How or why such similarities came to exist between European and Native American folklore is unknown.

If Passamaquoddy descriptions of water fairies in Maine are applicable to those living in New Hampshire, the water fairies here used magical pipes to produce enchanting music, utterly foreign to human ears. Their song could tame wild animals and entice human beings into sexual relationships, sometimes resulting in death. Occasionally, they'd give one of these pipes to a human, usually a great sorcerer or warrior, and thereby grant him the power of enchantment.

So if you're visiting Diana's Baths or Waternomee Falls, speak kindly of the Good Folk, stop up your ears and never accept their food, however enticing it may appear. Otherwise you may find yourself trapped in the forest forever, swimming endlessly in the mossy rock pools.

ONE LAST STORY FROM the White Mountains concerns an Abenaki family living near the headwater of the Ellis River, which rises east of Mount Washington and tumbles south through mountainous terrain, forming waterfalls and crystal pools. The family in question had a beautiful daughter whom every young man in the region desired. One day, the woman went out walking in the woods beside the river and never returned. Her parents looked for her everywhere, to no avail: nobody knew where she'd gone.

A few days later, a local hunter appeared at the parents' door saying he'd seen their daughter standing up to her waist in a pool in the Ellis River. She was embracing a strange-looking man he'd never seen before. Like the woman, the man had long hair that fell to his waist and fanned out on the surface of the water. Expecting the parents to receive the news with anxiety, the hunter was surprised to see their sadness mingled with relief. They said the man was one of the mountain spirits. He must have taken their daughter for a bride. Although their sadness was great because they knew they'd never see her again, they knew she was in a safe place now, destined to live forever with the spirits of the mountain.

Waterfall and pool along the Ellis River where legend says a mountain spirit took a beautiful Abenaki woman to be his partner. *Author's photo.*

Although the mountain spirit never revealed himself to the parents, the couple came to think of him as a kind of son-in-law. They left offerings beside the river for their daughter and the spirit, and the spirit reciprocated, leaving game for them to eat at their door. When the parents' time came to leave this world, they drew comfort from the fact that their daughter and her lover would forever inhabit the land around the Ellis River.

Although the parents described their daughter's lover as a spirit, his human form suggests he was what we might call a fairy. Many fairies in folklore throughout history have formed intimate relationships with humans, especially in the British and Irish traditions. One example is the story of a nineteenth-century Scottish man called Lachlann who, after falling in love with a fairy woman, exhausted himself trying to satisfy her needs and soon became afraid of her. To escape her, he left Scotland for Nova Scotia, but he soon wrote home to say his fairy lover had followed him there! In northern New England too, members of the Passamaquoddy tribe believed the Little People could transform themselves into beautiful men and women and inspire lust in human beings.

FAIRY FOOTPRINTS IN CAMPTON

The following story, collected in the early twentieth century, is unusual among New England fairy stories because it features a woman of English colonial stock who not only believed in fairies but also taught that belief to her children and grandchildren. Similar to the residents of Marblehead, Massachusetts, who bucked the Puritan trend of not believing in fairies, what we have here is perhaps an example of English fairy lore being passed down from colonial New England to the nineteenth-century inhabitants of Campton, New Hampshire.

In the 1830s, a woman called Mary Locke Woodman lived with her husband, Isaac, on a farm in the village of Campton in the foothills of the White Mountains. Mary had ten children, of whom only a few still lived at home when the events described in the story took place. Her second-youngest child, a boy of about eight years old, was called Charles. As I've already mentioned, Mary descended, on both sides, from English colonists with roots in New Hampshire going back to the seventeenth century. She also believed in fairies, a trait she'd acquired from her mother (who, incidentally, descended from residents of the well-known fairy hotspots of Devon and Somerset in South West England).

One day, Mary sent her son Charles into the field to tend to the cows. Although young, Charles had grown up on the farm and was used to this kind of labor: in those days, everybody helped run the family business. Hardly any time had passed, however, when the boy returned, breathless and excited, talking about a "beautiful little creature" he'd seen crossing the brook into the field. The creature, he said, had left tiny footprints in the soil.

As soon as she heard this, Mary lifted the baby she was nursing (whose name is unfortunately lost) and beckoned to her daughter Mary Ann to come with her. They followed Charles through the woods and down to the brook, and sure enough, there were the little creature's footprints impressed in the soil. Taking her baby, Mary lifted him up above the row of footprints and, choosing the clearest, deepest footprint, put one of his feet into the middle of it. Amazed, they saw that the foot almost perfectly matched the print.

Many years later, after Mary had passed away, her daughter Mary Ann related the events of that day to her own daughter Ellen. "People nowadays don't believe in fairies," she said, "but I tell you there were fairies."

One interesting aspect of this story is the emphasis on the fairy's physicality, particularly its feet, which are able to leave an impression in soil. This differs from other accounts of New Hampshire fairies, such as those of Dora Kunz—who believed fairy bodies were composed of "pure feeling"—and those suggesting fairies are as insubstantial as light (see the summary of the Fairy Census at the end of this chapter).

The portrayal of a physical being possessing a somewhat weighty body is consistent with elements of European and Native American folklore, but it also contradicts the notion that fairies could pass through material boundaries such as doors and windows. Fairy lore is nothing if not contradictory and probably shouldn't be understood as a coherent body of thought: it's not inconceivable that fairies could possess physical bodies while also having the ability to pass through physical matter, whether by making themselves extremely small or turning into a gaseous substance. As the Reverend Robert Kirk, seventeenth-century expert on Scottish fairies, once wrote: fairies have "bodies of congealed air" that "can enter into any cranny or cleft of the earth."

Perhaps the most mysterious thing about fairies is that nobody has ever been able to provide definitive information about them, leaving it to individuals and families to interpret their experiences as they see fit. Even the aesthetic impression fairies create cannot be neatly summarized: some are "beautiful," as in the case of Charles's fairy, while others are clearly ugly, as can be seen in the following story.

THE GREEN FAIRY OF DERRY

On December 15, 1956, Alfred Horne, who lived on Berry Road in a rural part of Derry, went out into the woods near his home to harvest the spruce that grew abundantly thereabouts. His plan was to sell the spruce as Christmas trees, and so he set off. When he reached the wood, he walked deep into the trees and began to pursue his festive goal, selecting the best trees and sawing them at the base. After a while, catching his breath, he looked up into the sky, and there, to his surprise, was a green creature, about two feet in height, "neither human nor animal," with large, lidless eyes, droopy ears and wrinkly skin that seemed to hang from a wiry frame—rather like an elephant's hide.

Alfred and the creature watched each other for about twenty minutes until Alfred thought it might be a good idea to catch it. He couldn't leave the wood without some tangible proof of what he'd seen or nobody would ever believe him, he thought. After lunging at the creature and missing, Alfred stepped back. Suddenly, the creature emitted a piercing scream. The sound was so terrifying, Alfred bolted. He didn't even stop to collect the trees he'd cut.

Derry historian Richard Holmes deserves credit for uncovering the strange tale's backstory. Before Holmes filled in the gaps, Joseph Citro had shared the story in his book *Weird New England* but had left Alfred Horne unnamed. Besides providing the protagonist's name, Holmes identified where the story originated: Alfred had mentioned the experience in a letter he'd sent, six years after the event occurred, to Boston-based astronomer and UFO expert Walter Webb. Apparently, Alfred had thought the creature was some kind of alien rather than a fairy, though everybody since has seemed content to call it the Derry Fairy.

Perhaps the most interesting thing about the story is how it calls into question the interpretive categories we use to identify phenomena, whether fairies or aliens. Alfred Horne isn't the only person to draw attention to the similarities between fairy folklore and modern-day descriptions of UFO sightings or "Little Green Men." Joseph Citro has also pointed out that stories about fairies and UFOs contain more or less similar motifs, including Little People, bright lights and the color green. One might even wonder whether the modern phenomenon of UFOs is a repackaging of ancient fairy beliefs.

As for Alfred's description of the Derry Fairy, readers can decide for themselves whether they think a fairy or an alien was lurking in the woods that day. While Alfred's description fits that of a stereotypical extraterrestrial, it also evokes uglier types of fairy such as the goblin or bogle.

SUMMARY OF THE FAIRY CENSUS
FOR NEW HAMPSHIRE

The New Hampshire–based entries in the Fairy Census of 2014–2017 reveal three visually fascinating encounters with fairies, two of which took place near woodlands, the other in someone's living room. In all three entries, the respondents described their experience as highly significant, two claiming it was a turning point in their lives.

The first response comes from a woman in her fifties who called her fairy encounter "the most remarkable thing" she'd ever seen. One night, she was lying on her couch after midnight when she saw lights coming along the hallway ceiling. Several winged fairies, she said, were traveling down the hallway, "almost dancing" near the ceiling and emitting a bright light. The fairies were so tiny, their "little bodies," she said, "would have been able to sit in my hand." At the same time, the woman was afraid: she felt sure she wasn't supposed to see what she was seeing. Finally, startled by a noise she must have made, the fairies flew hurriedly back the way they came.

In the second entry, a woman in her forties described waking up at 4:00 a.m. and looking out the window to see "multi-colored lights" dancing outside her home. Although she sensed something sinister about the lights, she felt a "longing" compelling her to go outside and be near them. This fear and longing combined inside her to create an "apathy for her personal safety." Eventually, the sun came up, and the lights vanished. The woman mentioned "a strange belief on my mother's Irish side of the family, that there is *sídhe* in our blood."

The third entry tells the story of a man in his twenties who was walking one fall afternoon in the woods when he stopped beside a brook. He crouched down in the sunlight next to the water and looked into a small pool. At that moment, "the quality of the light" appeared to change, the leaves seemed to fall more sluggishly and everything became quiet. When he looked up, he saw, about twenty feet away on the other side of the brook, a two-foot-tall "creature made all of leaves and sticks." The creature held a "walking staff" in one hand and had the "likeness of an old man, but composed entirely of leaves and twigs."

As in the first entry, the fairy looked distinctly unhappy about being seen; however, it seemed to understand that the man was well-intentioned. The man had just "inclined his head" as a mark of respect when the sound of a snapping twig distracted him. He looked away for an instant, and by the time he looked back, the creature had gone. The context for the story is that it took place at a site with a "reputation as a Native American living site, where artifacts had been recovered."

One interesting commonality of the stories is the role of light in the fairy experience. The first and second stories both involved fairies that appeared to emit light, suggesting the fairy species were similar. In the third story, the creature emitted no light and appeared to be more physical in nature. Although the man's perception of light did change right before he noticed the fairy, the fairy species appeared to be quite different.

As for the story about the woman whose Irish family believed they had sídhe (i.e., fairy) in their blood, her longing to go out and be close to the lights has clear parallels in Irish fairy folklore. In that tradition, the desire to be "away with the fairies" refers to a sickness-like craving for fairy company that takes away all interest in mortal life. Sometimes those who experience this malady have to be physically restrained to prevent them from wandering off to join the fairies. Or they may simply disappear and never return. The woman's description of her longing strongly evokes such traditions, especially in the context of her family's claim to possess sídhe blood.

5

RHODE ISLAND

Stories shared in this chapter are drawn from every corner of Rhode Island—from the rural northwest, where an Irish immigrant reported a vision of fearful banshees, to the South Coast, where fairies danced in the Matunuck Hills and Native American tribes spoke of a fairylike being singing sweet songs on the ocean-sprayed Sakonnet Point.

As early as the 1800s, one finds references in folklore to Rhode Islanders adopting magical practices such as "turning one's clothes" to ward off evil spirits. The practice, usually associated with fairies, involved turning one's coat inside out for protection. However, the largest influence on Rhode Island's fairy lore has undoubtedly been the mass Irish migration to the state that began in the mid-nineteenth century. Given the fact that Ireland was home to some of the richest and most deeply rooted fairy lore in Europe, it's no surprise that aspects of this lore traveled to New England with the Irish who migrated here.

Based on one Irish pastor's description of Providence's Irish residents in the 1850s—which will be covered in greater detail later in the chapter—it seems that the state's Irish American culture was fairly conservative, harkening back to customs that had begun to disappear even in Ireland. This means that Irish fairy lore in Rhode Island may have benefited from the rich cultural soil to be found here, which allowed it to flourish even under the disapproving gaze of the Catholic clergy and the Yankee authorities. Some of the beliefs about fairies and spirits associated with Irish lore have even survived into the present day.

Long before the Irish arrived in Rhode Island, the Native American tribes told stories about Little People who inhabited the hills and coastal regions of Narragansett Bay. The tribes who dwelled around the bay included the Narragansett, the Sakonnet and the Wampanoag; each had their respective folklore, though it was often quite similar. In this chapter, I share a story that a Wampanoag man told to an Englishman in 1792. I also make a hypothetical connection between the history of the Narragansett Tribe and a nineteenth-century folklorist's fanciful reference to fairies dancing in the Matunuck Hills.

THE LEGEND OF THE BANSHEE

The Irish of the eighteenth and nineteenth centuries often associated fairies with the dead. Spirits of lost loved ones populated the fairy Otherworld, and family members whom the fairies had "taken"—whether by drowning, stroke or a fit of madness—sometimes showed themselves in visions accompanied by the dead. Leaving food or milk outside one's home to placate the Good Folk was in many ways a similar practice to ancient ancestor worship found in traditions throughout the world, most notably in Rome. One of the most well-known fairies of Irish folklore, the banshee, may originally have functioned as an ancestral spirit attached to Irish families. Believers may have offered food to the banshee as an ancestral spirit in the hope she'd protect their kinsmen.

Perhaps it's a cliche to say this, but where the Irish go, the banshee follows. Therefore, it may not be a great surprise to learn that in Rhode Island, where Irish Americans make up the single largest ancestry group (more populous even than Italian Americans), the banshee's wail is a reported phenomenon.

The word *banshee* is a compound of two Irish Gaelic words, *bean* and *sídhe*, meaning "fairy woman" or "woman of the fairy mound." The banshee is known in folklore as a female spirit who attaches herself to a particular family and wails horribly (she *keens*) when a scion of that family is about to die. Legend suggests the banshee wails only for families of the purest Irish blood; in the case of North America, only families of unmixed Irish heritage can claim to have drawn the banshee with them across the sea. Hence, wealthy Irish Americans in Washington, D.C., and St. Louis, Missouri, wishing to emphasize their pedigree, have been known to claim descent from a "banshee family." Perhaps the thought that a banshee has followed one halfway around the world becomes oddly reassuring in a cultural context where everything is new—especially, one might add, when the world one left behind has been ravaged by sickness and death, as in the case of nineteenth-century Ireland.

New England author Joseph Citro likens the sound of the banshee's wail to feline caterwauling with an underbelly of human lamentation. Like many characteristics of the fae, the sound is uncanny, almost human but not quite. It starts out extraordinarily loud, making the hair on one's head stand up. It is so close, too, that it seems the fairy must be perched on the roof of one's house or standing at the door. Gradually it fades, as if the fairy is moving away—returning, perhaps, to the Otherworld from whence she came. The keening fills the heart and mind of the hearer—who, of course, knows someone close to him is about to die—with supernatural dread and awe. Death itself has penetrated the world of the living, and nobody is safe.

Stories of Irish interaction with fairies have traveled as far as Dubuque, Iowa, but the story I wish to share with you now concerns the successful Irish American owner of a New England supermarket chain. Joseph Citro shared the story in his book *Passing Strange*, and I mention it here because it serves as the perfect introduction to the next story featured in this chapter.

Early nineteenth-century depiction of a banshee from *Fairy Legends and Traditions of the South of Ireland* by Thomas Crofton Croker. *Public domain.*

Significantly, it suggests the banshee's wail may have haunted five generations of Irish New Englanders.

Generations ago in Boston, an Irishman who'd recently arrived in the New World set up a grocery store that eventually became the first in a chain of supermarkets spread throughout New England. One spring morning in the 1930s, the youngest member of this food-distribution empire awoke to a sound he could only compare to a "demented woman's" wailing. Although it sounded like a human woman, it filled his ears with an unholy resonance unlike anything he'd heard before. Immediately he got up and went downstairs to find his father crying in the living room, an unusual sight for this age-old Irish family. It was then he learned the patriarch of the family had died. His grandfather was no more.

It wasn't until many years later that the boy, now a successful businessman, learned about the legend of the banshee and realized he'd heard her wail.

The supernatural keening manifested itself to the man on two further occasions. When he was stationed in the Far East after the Second World War, he heard a "low howling" that progressed in volume until it was similar to an "air-raid siren," rising and falling in waves. This time, filled with sadness, he knew his father had died. A third time, he heard the banshee's wail when visiting Toronto on a business trip. Terrified that his wife or one of his children had died, he phoned home, but everything appeared to be fine. It turned out it was November 22, 1963—the day someone assassinated his dear friend, the former Irish American president John F. Kennedy.

The story I wish to share in this chapter on Rhode Island concerns another banshee-haunted Irish American, this time a woman by the name of Ellen Carson. It will be left up to the reader to decide if the banshees Ellen saw were literal fairies or the metaphorical embodiments of sickness and starvation. If Ellen's relatives are to be believed, she was sure of what she'd seen: banshees had visited her village.

THE BANSHEES OF HARRISVILLE

The tiny village of Harrisville lies in the secluded northwest corner of the Ocean State, almost on the Massachusetts state line. Despite its proximity to Providence (thirty minutes by car), the village today retains the sleepy atmosphere of an old nineteenth-century mill town. It displays its industrial origins in the form of a dam, over which the Clear River cascades out of

Old Stone Bridge over the Clear River in Harrisville, location of a nineteenth-century banshee sighting. *Author's photo.*

a large man-made pond. I came here to investigate the river's old bridge, reportedly the site of fairy hauntings in the late nineteenth century. Built in 1902, the stone bridge replaced a much older one of wood.

In the 1840s, Irish refugees, fleeing the Great Famine ravaging their homeland, arrived in Harrisville to work in the textile mill. The stream of immigrants—weakened by hunger, forced out by cruel evictions or escaping debts they couldn't pay—continued for many decades, giving Harrisville a very Irish flair. Many came from County Roscommon, where famine and forced evictions tragically destroyed or sent into exile 31 percent of the population over the course of ten years. Those who arrived in Harrisville found comfort at St. Patrick's Church and managed to create something of a sanctuary for themselves so many miles from home—until plague came, that is. In the 1850s, tuberculosis and cholera attacked the already famine-weakened immigrants, who soon began to fill Burrillville's St. Patrick's Cemetery with their loved ones.

Among the County Roscommon immigrants was a girl of fifteen called Ellen Gilroe, who arrived in Harrisville in 1872 in the aftermath of the famine and the worst of the cholera outbreaks. Born to Irish parents in Manchester, England (she identified as English all her life), she was raised in Ireland and for a time lived with her mother in a County Roscommon workhouse, a place where the very poor worked for accommodation and food rations. Upon her arrival in America, it's likely she went to work in the Stillwater Woolen Mill on the Clear River, and in 1879, she married an Irishman, Francis Carson, with whom she had seven children. Thanks to memories shared through three generations, we know that Ellen, or Nellie, as her family called her, was something of a fairy seer.

Not everyone has the dubious luck of being able to see fairies. In the case of the banshee, those who are able to see them might rather wish they hadn't. For the type of banshee whose wail is a prophecy of death is unlikely to be one of those shining beings or fairy maidens sometimes reported in Irish folklore. That type of fairy—who's also a banshee (the word, as we've learned, means "fairy woman")—is far more likely to be a seducer of men, a succubus who bears fairy children to mortals. The banshee who prophesies death, on the other hand, is far more likely to be a gray-haired crone wrapped in a mantle, an otherworldly mist surrounding her. Her blood-curdling screech and tear-stained cheeks express all the horror and despair of encroaching death.

According to Ellen's great-grandson Ray McKenna, who writes about Rhode Island's Irish American history on his blog *Federal Hill Irish*, the losses of the Great Famine forever haunted Ellen. Given that her earliest childhood memories were of Ireland in the famine's aftermath, this perhaps comes as no surprise. Ellen bore the wounds of loss and death until her own death came in 1939. "She could never come to grips with the horror the famine years brought to the family," wrote Ray. When those horrors continued in

Ellen Gilroe Carson, who saw banshees coming over the bridge into Harrisville in the nineteenth century. *Photo courtesy of Ray McKenna.*

the form of tuberculosis and cholera, the trauma this entailed apparently gave Ellen a unique vision of the spirit world. At some point during her time in Harrisville, she claimed to have seen banshees coming over the old wooden bridge into the village, a fact Ray learned from his grandmother, Ellen's daughter.

It should be pointed out that most visitors to Harrisville pass over the bridge into the village, especially those arriving from the more populous parts of Rhode Island near Providence. Hence, the bridge is not just a physical entry point but also a symbolic one. Just as one's front door is the entry point to one's home, the bridge over Clear River is the entry point to the Harrisville community. For this reason, it seems natural that if banshees were to come to Harrisville, they would do so from this direction, no other entry point having the same symbolic weight. (It should be noted, however, that in Irish lore, fairies are sometimes incapable of crossing running water, and one way to escape from them when they're in pursuit is to cross over a brook or stream.)

But did Ellen really see banshees? To play the devil's advocate, I might suggest she used a figure of speech, the banshee being the perfect metaphor for her fear of approaching death. In the book *Magical Folk*, Chris Woodyard pointed out that at some point in the history of Irish folklore, "the term 'banshee' eventually ceased to signify a warning spirit attached to a family and became a generic token of death." After hundreds of years of Irish people using the word to signify a death-foretelling fairy, the word became detached from its literal meaning and became a way to talk about death in general. To claim that banshees were coming over the bridge was one way to say that death was on its way. We know that death's insistence haunted Ellen, first during the Great Famine and then over the course of years of community sickness. Perhaps she meant to imply that death had come—a fact that would have been impossible to deny in late nineteenth-century Harrisville, when it prowled the streets in waves.

So let me ask the question again before allowing Ellen's great-grandson Ray to answer it: Was Ellen Carson speaking metaphorically?

Not so, says Ray. He is in no doubt that Ellen was speaking literally. "My great-grandmother saw banshees," he explained to me in an email. "She was sure of it."

To put Ellen's beliefs in their proper context, Ray drew my attention to Irishman James Donnelly's monthslong visit to Providence in 1854, when he described the city's Irish residents in detail. Donnelly, a priest and later bishop of Clogher, had a great love for his fellow Irish men and women, but he was also wary of anything that might serve to reinforce Americans' anti-Irish sentiment. The native superstitions and disorderly behaviors he witnessed among Providence's Irish immigrants, including women grieving publicly and men fighting, horrified him. These immigrants often came from the rural west of Ireland, counties such as Ellen Carson's Roscommon, where conservative and superstitious practices survived longer and where people were more likely to engage in traditions such as public keening or making fairy offerings. As someone who'd spent most of her childhood in a western county, Ellen might well have held on to a strong belief in fairies, especially given the fact that traditional Irish culture seemed to have survived for so long in Rhode Island.

Besides, Ellen wasn't the only member of her family to see fairies. They say the propensity to see them is a gift of the Irish, and Ellen, it seems, passed the trait to her Irish American descendants. "In my own family," Ray wrote, "belief in the otherworld survives beyond my great-grandmother's banshee experience." The spirits were known to visit Ray's grandmother, his mother, and two relatives of his own generation, a phenomenon not unusual for those with Irish heritage. "I don't think they are unique in Rhode Island," he explained, "or anywhere that the Irish diaspora cast its spell. Call them ghosts, call them fairies, what will you, they persevere."

THE IRISH FAIRY FAITH IN THE OCEAN STATE

Walking in St. Patrick's Cemetery in Providence among the graves of the city's famine-era Irish, one notices a number of hawthorn trees growing among the stones. The gnarled branches and hollowed-out trunks of these ancient thorns make it fairly easy to see why the Irish, in times gone by, called them *fairy trees*: their hollows look like underworld portals accessible only to miniature beings.

When Ray McKenna visited the cemetery a few years ago with the County Monaghan historian Larry McDermott, Larry explained to him the significance of the hawthorn and why it should be planted in an Irish Catholic cemetery:

For the ancient Irish, the tree symbolized, above all things, hope. Tradition said the crown of thorns placed on Jesus's head was gathered from a hawthorn, and for this reason, the tree represented the mystical union between this world and the next. The lone hawthorn standing in the middle or edge of a field was often called a fairy tree because it acted as a gateway to the Otherworld. Even for the most hardened atheist, the sight of a single twisted thorn in the middle of a farmer's field, standing firm through centuries of wind and rain, impresses the mind with a sense of spiritual resilience. Perhaps this is why the tree was called sacred to the fairies, and why cutting or felling one was considered sacrilege. In fact, desecration of a hawthorn tree was thought to bring down a terrible misfortune on the one who committed it, the offended fairies seeking revenge.

On his blog, Ray McKenna shares two fascinating stories from County Tyrone that help us understand the fairy faith of the Irish immigrants who planted the hawthorns of St. Patrick's Cemetery. Large-scale migration from

One of many hawthorn trees found in St. Patrick's Cemetery in Providence. *Author's photo.*

Tyrone to Providence took place in the nineteenth century, making it likely that the mystical ideas contained in these stories reflected the beliefs and superstitions of at least some of Rhode Island's Irish residents. Belief in the sanctity of hawthorns was prevalent in Tyrone, and local people generally knew not to disturb a fairy tree due to the risk of a terrible reprisal. One farming family learned this the hard way when their maidservant took some dead branches from a hawthorn tree to kindle the fire in their home. As soon as the maid set the branches on fire, one of the family's cows fell sick. They were only able to restore the cow to health when the master of the house ordered the maidservant to return the branches to the foot of the tree. Another story from the same region involved a married couple called Mickey and Ann Fairish who cut down a thorn tree to build their home's foundations. That night, three small men entered the couple's home unbidden and warned them of the dire consequences if they didn't return the land to its original state. Obeying, the couple were rewarded for their compliance with a bag of tobacco, a gift from the fairies. Although no stories as dramatic as these have survived in Rhode Island, the beliefs expressed in the stories must have arrived, at some point, on these shores. They possibly underpin the practice we turn our attention to now.

Besides their belief in banshees and their likely reverence of fairy trees, nineteenth-century Rhode Islanders also demonstrated their fairy faith when they adopted Old World charms to ward off fairy attacks. This can be seen in two early-nineteenth-century references to people "turning their clothes" in the state. Common throughout Ireland and Britain, the practice involved turning one's coat inside out when walking home at night to protect oneself against malicious spirits. Doing so was said to confuse the fairies and prevent them from leading you astray. Sometimes it was enough simply to turn out the pockets of one's coat to keep the fairies at bay. The book *In Old Narragansett* mentions two Rhode Islanders, a man and a woman, walking at night with their clothes "turned"—he with his waistcoat and she with her petticoat— to relieve their fear of spirits. Such practices, learned from ancestors, clearly survived the ocean voyage and became established in the state.

A word should be said here about the American Catholic clergy's response to the Irish fairy faith, for the clergy played an important role in shaping the dissemination of folklore. Historian Chris Woodyard has pointed out that priests and bishops in the nineteenth century endeavored to put a stop to all types of superstitious beliefs among Irish Americans. Perhaps unsurprisingly, the Catholic clergy had a lot of influence over the types of folklore that would be transmitted to the New World, and their priority was for parishioners to adapt to the rational, orderly values of their adopted home. This found impetus in the fact that many priests, being middle class, wished to maintain the American way of life rather than revert to Old World behaviors. The fairy faith and its associated practices were hardly compatible with secular values that celebrated humanism and rejected magical thinking. Many Americans, particularly community leaders, found the notion that "We, the People" might be subject to unpredictable influences such as fairies abhorrent or laughable. The Church, of course, took note.

History suggests the clergy's campaign to "enlighten" Irish Americans was quite successful, as folklore about fairies remained fairly inconspicuous throughout the nineteenth century. The immigrants' own desire to integrate into American life aided the Church in its campaign to eradicate superstitious beliefs. This probably explains the relatively sporadic nature of references to fairies in New England, despite the examples we've seen so far. Nevertheless, the fact that priests, in historian Kerby Miller's words, continued to condemn "traditional wakes, fairy belief…crossroads dancing, and all other practices which threatened either clerical or bourgeois hegemony," suggests some Irish immigrants held on to old ideas despite the Church's protestations. Certainly, the "turning of clothes" and belief in banshees remained prevalent in Rhode Island for some time.

So if you ever visit Providence's St. Patrick's Cemetery and spy the hawthorn trees growing among the graves, say a prayer, perhaps, for the Irish immigrants who planted these trees beside the bodies of their loved ones. Then, turn out the pockets of your coat and be careful what you say: a fairy could be waiting in the hollow of a thorn, listening to your every word.

THE FAIRIES OF THE MATUNUCK HILLS

Leaving Rhode Island's Irish enclaves behind, I traveled south to the lands of the Narragansett Tribe to investigate a reference to fairies in one of the state's most mysterious and secluded places: the Matunuck Hills. This wooded, undulating region, which glaciers formed many thousands of years ago, lies north of the coastal village of Matunuck, the former site of a Native American encampment. Nearer the sea, Rhode Island's forests become denser, and like the trails between the trees, the fairy lore becomes more difficult to illuminate.

The authors Chris Woodyard and Simon Young recently included a reference to fairies inhabiting this part of Rhode Island in a list of North

American fairy experiences worth investigating. The reference appeared in the work of Thomas Robinson Hazard, an author and folklorist, who, in the 1880s, wrote that fairies "used to congregate and dance by moonlight in the olden time" in the Matunuck Hills. The reference is a mysterious one because no other literary or historical sources appear to mention such a legend.

The hills in question—fairy haunted or not—rise up behind the coastal village of Matunuck in the southern portion of the state. One lush forest dotted with ponds and the occasional home, the Hills are accessed via a private road that opens up into a grassy clearing once called Hovel Hollow. The sheep that pastured here are gone now, and a solitary silver birch stands in the middle of the clearing. Two centuries ago, acres of blooming rhododendrons and mountain laurel covered these hills, and even now, small clumps of the native plants remain. As one enters the wood, the region's astonishing quietness becomes apparent: birdsong and the rustle of chipmunks are all that break the silence. One feels one has entered an enchanted world.

Despite the location's fairylike beauty, Thomas Robinson Hazard's reference to the hills' fairies seems at first to be a poetic conceit, a way to emphasize the region's unspoiled beauty, not meant to be taken literally. When he said that fairies danced here in the moonlight, surely he meant to emphasize the spot's natural wildness rather than its supernatural inhabitants? I'm not so sure. The more I considered the type of man Hazard was—a spiritualist quite capable of believing in fairies—the more I began to wonder if his reference to hillside dancers was based on something more concrete.

Could it be that Hazard referred to an old, unfortunately now-forgotten legend, perhaps a story of the Narragansett Tribe?

We know the Narragansetts occupied the coastline beneath these hills and used them as a lookout over the Narragansett Bay. The word *matunuck* in fact means "lookout" in the old Narragansett language and probably refers to the hills themselves. We also know they visited the region's Hot House Pond to sit in the water, smoke tobacco and apply hot stones to their bodies as a way to purge disease. Roger Williams, Rhode Island's founder, attests to this practice in his writings on the Narragansett language. Other ponds, too, such as White Pond, speak to a Narragansett presence in these hills: the pond's *whiteness*, as they saw it, refers to the water's clarity, which so perfectly reflected the light on cloudy days that the water resembled a large white sheet.

As to whether the Narragansett Tribe believed that magical beings inhabited these hills so close to their coastal settlement, it seems highly likely. An Algonquian-speaking tribe, the Narragansett shared many stories with their northeastern tribal neighbors. They worshiped a deity similar to Granny Squannit, whom they called Squauanit. Like the Mohegans and the Wampanoag, they believed that giants inhabited the land: their stories about a giant called Wetucks resemble other nations' stories about Maushop. As for the Little People, Lorén Spears, a former tribal councilwoman of the Narragansett Tribe, told me in an email that Little People are "very much part of our oral tradition," although no specific ancient references to them have survived. Nevertheless, it seems quite possible that the Narragansett believed the Little People dwelled quietly in these hills. Few places in Rhode Island provide a home for them as secluded as here.

Did Thomas Robinson Hazard mean to evoke an ancient Native American legend when he claimed the fairies danced here? Although we'll probably never know, I did find myself stopping at the entrance to a strangely tiny trail leading down to Cedar Swamp Pond, overhung with branches: the trail's size and the branches' height seemed perfect for a two-foot person, almost as if it was fairy-made. If that isn't enough to convince you of the fairy-haunted nature of these hills, the beautiful seclusion of the place just might.

THE SIREN OF SAKONNET POINT

Heading east over Conanicut and Aquidneck Island, I arrived at Sakonnet Point, a ribbon of land extending a short way into the Atlantic Ocean. I'd come to investigate a fairylike being whose life among the rocks and seagulls of the Point is the focus of the final story in this chapter. Visiting in summer, I found wild swamp roses blooming along the strip of land and an ocean that sparkled on either side of gleaming sand. In every direction, the unspoiled prospect evoked what New England must have been when members of the area's neighboring tribes canoed in the surrounding waters.

The story of Sakonnet Point's fairy first appeared in 1792 when a Wampanoag man called Thomas Cooper, who lived at Gay Head on Martha's Vineyard, shared it with an Englishman called Benjamin Bassett. Cooper himself had learned the story from his elderly grandmother. The narrative's antiquity is evident from the fact that the grandmother herself remembered the English Puritans arriving in 1643, suggesting the story of Sakonnet Point has deep roots in Wampanoag culture.

Sakonnet Point in Southern Rhode Island, where Maushop's wife lived and was turned to stone. *Author's photo.*

It's clear from the story that not every fairy woman found in Rhode Island emits an unpleasant sound like the banshee's keening. In one version of the story, which may well have diverged from Thomas Cooper's original, she's actually known for her beautiful song.

Long ago when the Narragansett, Wampanoag and Sakonnet Tribes occupied Rhode Island's Narragansett Bay and the friendly giant Maushop lived in the land, Maushop's wife, Squant (a tiny woman with a rabbit-sized foot, whom we read about in the chapters on Connecticut and Massachusetts), couldn't stop crying because her husband had turned their sons into killer whales. Unable to stand the sound of her grief for another minute, Maushop grabbed Squant by the hair and threw her high into the air.

When the poor woman came crashing down, she realized she was lying among the rocks of Sakonnet Point. Squant stayed on the Point for the rest of her life, exacting tribute from the men and women who paddled in the ocean. Eventually, the Great Spirit turned her into a stone, and the English, who feared the return of her powers, kept breaking off pieces of rock to weaken her. The story may have functioned as a warning to Wampanoag wives not to anger their husbands. It can also be interpreted as a critique of the English, the destruction of the rock representing their theft of land and suppression of divine powers.

A later version of the tale appears in the work of folklorist Ellen Russell Emerson, who apparently embellished the tale, giving the woman a melancholy singing voice that filled the bay with its sound. In this version, the woman's sorrow was so profound and her singing gave such relief, she could hardly bring herself to move from the Point. Wampanoag men and women, sailing their canoes in the shallow water, drew close to hear her bewitching voice. Pulling up to the shore, they listened with wonder to the swelling notes. The woman became known as the Siren of Narragansett Bay because her voice was so irresistibly sweet, an apparent addition to the story based on Homer's *Odyssey*. Every day she requested tribute from the men and women who came to listen, drawn by her song's hypnotic power. Every day, they brought her baskets of corn and tobacco, and every day, she sang.

In this later version of the story, too, the woman remained on the Point for so long, she eventually turned into a rock.

6

VERMONT

Vermont is home to some of New England's most remote and inaccessible terrain, so it's no surprise that fairies and fairylike beings lurk undisturbed in the woodlands and swamps here. Unlike other New England states, however, historical reports of fairy beliefs and encounters appear to be entirely Native American in origin. While nineteenth-century Vermonters left evidence of their belief in witches, vampires, the devil and angelic visitations, they seem not to have thought much about fairies. This is despite the fact that Sir Arthur Conan Doyle, one of the most famous fairy believers in history, visited the state in the 1890s and took an active interest in spiritualism here. Unfortunately, Doyle failed to bring to light any Vermont fairies, leaving us with only Native American stories to occupy our interest. This is no bad thing in itself: the Native American bands who occupied the Vermont region—called the Western Abenaki to distinguish them from the Abenaki who inhabited Maine—had a fascinating worldview, full of magical beings and nature-dwelling spirits.

For thousands of years before the French and English arrived in Vermont, the Western Abenaki and their constituent bands lived in family groupings, each connected to a shared village culture in the Lake Champlain Valley. The Abenaki families used the lake and local creeks to navigate the area in birchbark canoes, forming settlements beside the water and along the northerly Missisquoi River. On the other side of the lake, the magnificent Adirondack Mountains signaled the end of the Abenakis' domain and the beginning of enemy territory, for the Iroquois who lived there belonged to a different people and an alternative tribal confederacy.

The Abenaki inhabited a world they often explained through stories. Although no Scientific Revolution comparable to the scholarly transformations seen in Europe during the sixteenth and seventeenth centuries had occurred among them, they possessed a knowledge and understanding of land, food, medicine and animals that was far greater than that of the Europeans who eventually came here. Stories occupied a particularly useful place in this knowledge, especially when it came to navigating the dangerous woodlands and wetlands of their home. According to the historians Marjory Power and William Haviland, Abenaki tales about the dangers of the local landscape included stories about frozen lakes and swamps. If a patch of ice in a frozen lake in the depths of winter was inexplicably thinner than the rest of the lake, the Abenaki would associate that patch with a malicious spirit looking to drown a tribal member. If a man disappeared while hunting in the Green Mountains, some malevolent creature must have got him. Similarly, swamps and marshes teemed with spirits waiting for the Abenaki to become stuck in the mud.

While researching the stories in this chapter, I couldn't help thinking about the extent to which we, in the modern world, expect scientifically plausible explanations for almost everything we encounter. In comparison, as Power and Haviland pointed out, the Abenaki worldview had "a fairy tale quality about it," incorporating magical stories. Of course, the Abenaki didn't view their stories as mere fairy tales. They intended them to be pragmatic and useful explanations of the facts of nature. For example, by ascribing supernatural activity to real and potent dangers, they ensured family members took proper precautions when traversing the land. Just as we in the modern era tell our children ancient fairy tales to teach them moral lessons, so the Abenaki shared their stories to instruct the young. In this chapter, we'll investigate some of these stories, including the tale of the *manogemassak* or Little People who left strange artifacts in a Lake Champlain bay, and spirits who wailed from the bulrushes in the marshes.

THE MANOGEMASSAK

In the chapter on Maine, we met the oonohgamesuk, or water fairies, whose name among the New England Algonquian tribes had many variations. We also learned in the chapter on New Hampshire that, according to folklorist Charles Leland, the pools and waterfalls of Diana's Baths near North

Conway were originally named after these diminutive beings. In Vermont, the Western Abenaki knew these beings as manogemassak. The notion that these names refer to the same being arises from their linguistic similarity and the fact that the beings in question behave in similar ways. For example, Vermont's manogemassak and Maine's wenagameswook both created clay figures and left them beside rivers and lakes for the Abenaki to find. That two apparently separate mythological beings would exhibit identical behavior is not particularly surprising: the northeastern tribes were always culturally and linguistically similar.

The water fairies of Vermont—whose name translates more precisely as "Little People"—lived underwater in deep pools in rivers and lakes. Like their kin in other New England states, they tended to avoid human contact and did not like to be seen. Similar to Maine's wenagameswook, they had thin faces, which historians Power and Haviland described as "like axe blades," and they spoke in "small, squeaky voices." The fairies traversed the Lake Champlain Valley's creeks and marshes in stone canoes, alongside but usually invisible to the Abenaki. If the Abenaki did see them, the manogemassak immediately submerged their canoes and disappeared. Generally, they behaved in a friendly way toward the Abenaki, only sometimes capsizing their canoes or destroying their fishing nets. They were particularly busy at night, for then they went to work building clay figures, which they left on the banks of rivers and lakes. The Abenaki believed that finding these figures brought them luck.

What exactly were these clay figures? In fact, they're natural artifacts called concretions, and they often took forms the Abenaki thought resembled animals and humans. Concretions are made when mud or clay from a riverbed or lake clumps around a small rock, shell or plant. When calcium hardens the clay, it forms interesting symmetrical and asymmetrical shapes. Sometimes these shapes are so intricate and artificial looking, they could easily be mistaken for artistic molds. In the case of plant concretions, after the clay adheres to the plant matter, the plant dies, leaving behind a concrete-clay "button" with a hole in the middle where the plant's stem was. Many such buttons have been discovered at Button Bay on Lake Champlain's eastern shore.

When the Abenaki found these concretions and attributed their artistic-looking qualities to the water fairies' nighttime activities, they demonstrated their reliance on stories—in other words, the use of a tale about supernatural beings to explain processes that, today, we would consider geological. In this sense, the Abenaki lived in a world in which geology and magic overlapped.

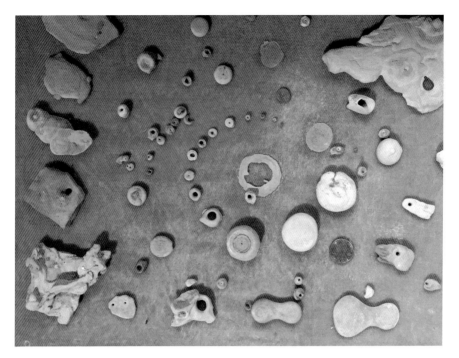

Clay concretions found at Button Bay on Lake Champlain. The Abenaki believed that the water fairies made them. *Button Bay State Park.*

In order to gain a better understanding of what it meant to live in a world inhabited by magical beings, one might wish to visit Button Bay and walk through the forest to Button Point. The experience comes close to magical, and the point itself, curling out into the lake, offers magnificent, almost 360-degree views of Lake Champlain, the Adirondacks forming the backdrop. A full-time interpreter whose job it is to help people understand the area's geological and historical significance works at the Bay. She can also show you the water fairies' unusual artifacts. One may come away with a greater understanding of the Abenakis' world of stories.

Incidentally, concretions similar to those found at Button Bay have also been found at Fort Hill, a fortified Sokoki settlement near Hinsdale, New Hampshire, close to the Vermont border. The Sokoki—an Abenaki band who lived in the Connecticut River Valley but who maintained close contact with the Lake Champlain bands—probably found many concretions on the shores of the Connecticut and attributed their formation to the water fairies who lived in the river. In the chapter on New Hampshire, we encountered a story about the Sokoki and the water fairies of Diana's Baths, so it's likely

The end of Button Point at Button Bay on Lake Champlain, legendary home of the water fairies of Abenaki folklore. *Author's photo.*

this branch of the Abenaki family shared their neighbors' beliefs regarding Little People and clay concretions. As the archaeologist Peter A. Thomas pointed out, Sokoki beliefs about the "fundamental nature of the physical and supernatural environment" likely underwent "little change" between the precolonial and postcolonial period.

SWAMP SPIRITS

From as early as they could remember, Abenaki children grew up hearing about swamp spirits who dwelled in the Lake Champlain Valley's wetlands. Entering the valley through a huge pass in the Green Mountains, one comes to a large area of mainly flat or gently rolling land covered in boggy creeks, marshes and swamps. This is the terrain the Abenaki navigated with their children; hence, it paid to warn the little ones where they could and couldn't go. Swamps were certainly no-go areas, and the storytelling about them was endless. As Power and Haviland pointed out, for the Abenaki, storytelling "was a favorite pastime, and so every child growing up heard over and over myths and tales detailing the exploits of all the various supernatural beings."

Vermont's swamp spirits were similar in many ways to British and Irish fairies who lured people into wetlands to do them harm. While European fairies used glowing lights to achieve this end, Abenaki spirits usually called out to passersby in an eerie voice. The Abenaki spirits also differed in that stories about them were intimately connected with Abenaki child-rearing. This had to do with the role of storytelling in the Abenaki culture, which often stood in for harsher means of disciplining children. While the patriarchal families of European immigrants subjected children to the father's strict authority, Abenaki families were fairly hands-off with their children. Rather than smacking or scolding them, Abenaki elders preferred to educate their young through positive examples and constant telling of stories.

This is where swamp spirits enter the picture, for swamps are inherently dangerous places, full of venomous snakes and often covered by a layer

Wetland in the Lake Champlain Valley, home of many swamp spirits, according to Abenaki legend. *Author's photo.*

of moss that appears to be firm but easily gives way. Dead and decaying plant matter gives the swamp a murkiness that almost seems bottomless, while gases produced by anaerobic bacteria occasionally bubble up, giving the impression that some living, breathing thing lurks beneath the water. Sometimes these gases burn on contact with the air, producing disorienting lights called will-o'-the-wisp. With this in mind, it's no surprise the Abenaki told their children terrifying stories about swamps.

The most common story told to children was that if they approached a swamp alone, they'd hear a spirit crying among the trees. If the child investigated the sound—thinking it was a human person—the spirit would drown them.

In some Abenaki tales, swamp spirits took a more personal form, appearing as a fairylike being called Skwakowtemus, meaning "Swamp Woman." Skwakowtemus wore moss and bark for clothes and had long, mossy hair. Her mournful cries lured children into swamps, where she'd drown them. Some Abenaki said she was the ghost of a woman who'd died childless. Full of good intentions, she called out to children because she was lonely. When they came to her, she'd cuddle them kindly, only to find they'd died in her arms. A sculptural representation of Skwakowtemus carved by Penobscot artist Tim Shay can be seen along a trail on Indian Island, the Penobscot reservation in Maine.

Another female spirit, probably originating in the same tale, was known as Pskegdemus. A lonely inhabitant of the swamps, she longed so much for male company and the presence of children, she made it her goal to lure lonesome hunters into the wetlands and never let them go. If a man thought about Pskegdemus with compassion, the thought alone would doom him to remain unmarried forever, while those who strongly desired to see her were said to experience a terrifying visitation. Clearly, it was best not to think about her at all.

One other personage inhabiting northern New England's swamps, attested by the Eastern Abenaki and probably known to the Western, was Maski'ksu, a name meaning "toad creature." Although described as a toad, Maski'ksu was usually depicted as a fairylike woman who, similar to the female swamp spirits, wore moss and bark for clothes and wailed mournfully around Abenaki villages, looking for a man or child she could hold. The anthropologist Frank Speck described her as a "seducer of men and children," for she longed for human touch. However, as soon as she got her wish, whomever she embraced fell into a deep sleep and died. One story goes that a man returned from a hunt to find Maski'ksu holding his child. His wife had given the baby to the woman out of compassion for her distress. Angrily, he took the child and drove Maski'ksu into the surrounding woods. In another story, four Penobscot men out trapping wild animals encountered Maski'ksu sitting on a grassy patch beside a stream, humming to herself. The men described her as having very dark skin and being about two and a half feet tall.

Not all of Vermont's swamp spirits were dangerous or threatening beings. The folklorist Charles Leland shared a myth associated with swamps that he claimed to have heard among the New England tribes. He said the grass-like sweet flags, which rise up out of the wetlands in multitudes, were thought to descend from swamp spirits. Sweet flags resemble cattails or bulrushes and can be seen in great numbers in the Lake Champlain Valley. The Abenaki called them muskrat plants because they often saw the muskrats digging up and eating the plant's rhizomes. As well as harvesting the plant for medicine, the Abenaki used it as bait, muskrats being an important source of meat and fur. If Leland's reporting of Algonquian myth is to be believed, the Abenaki harbored a reverential attitude toward the sweet flag, and evidence suggests bunches of it could be found throughout Abenaki villages, where it was used for all manner of purposes.

A WILL O' TH' WISP: OR JACK O'LANTERN!

A late eighteenth-century depiction of a fairy will-o'-the-wisp leading a man and woman into a marsh near a churchyard. *Public domain*.

The belief that swamp spirits were the ancestors of the sweet flag can be seen reflected in another legend recorded by Frank Speck. In the story, a being from the swamps visited an Eastern Abenaki man in a dream and identified himself as the spirit of the muskrat plant. At that time, many Penobscot tribe members were dying of cholera, and the spirit had come to teach the man how to heal the sick using the sweet flag's roots. He took the man to a swamp and showed him where the sweet flag grew. When the man woke from his dream, he went to the swamp and gathered the plant's roots, which he made into medicine to heal the Penobscot. The story suggests that swamps in Abenaki folklore attracted various types of fairylike spirits, both malicious and kind.

Interestingly, the Abenaki preoccupation with swamp spirits strongly agrees with European stories about swamp-dwelling fairies such as will-o'-the-wisp, a malicious lantern-carrying being who lured unsuspecting passersby to a watery doom. Many stories from Southern England concern pixies leading people into swamps, while the nineteenth-century poet John Clare was said to have experienced fairy pinches and blows in a swampy location between two Cambridgeshire villages. The difference between Abenaki stories and their English counterparts is that the former tell of spirits who cry mournfully, while the latter concern mischievous beings who snigger when they lure a walker into a pond or marsh. Fear of swamps appears to be universal.

THE CORN MOTHER

The final, extremely gruesome story in this chapter concerns a beautiful female spirit somewhat difficult to define: Is she a fairy inhabiting the natural world or an earth goddess incarnate in human flesh? Similar to the sweet flag myth, this legend depicts a fairylike being as the flesh-and-blood ancestor of corn. Told by the Eastern Abenaki, the story—or some variant of it—was probably familiar to the Vermont region's Abenaki as well. It should be remembered that the Abenaki held corn in high regard because it was a staple food in their diet. This possibly explains the story's depiction of the plant as possessing supernatural origins.

The story begins at some primordial point in history when the region's lakes and rivers had dried up, causing the Abenaki to starve for want of food. As if out of nowhere, a beautiful woman appeared in an Abenaki village and married one of the men who lived there. After a while, the man noticed his wife kept disappearing for long periods of time. One day he followed her into the woods and found she'd been meeting secretly with her lover, who was a snake. When he confronted the woman about her infidelity, she told him she'd come to fulfill an important mission that would benefit the Abenaki. She took him to a clearing in the woods and told him to kill her with a stone axe. "When this is done," she said, "you must drag my body around the clearing until the flesh is stripped from my bones. Bury my bones in the middle of the clearing and then return to your wigwam. Wait for seven days without returning. If you do this, I promise everyone in the land will eat."

The man did everything the woman said and returned to his wigwam. When the seven days had passed, he went back to the clearing and found that where the woman's blood had fallen, corn had sprung up. Looking closely at the corn's yellow leaves, he saw an image of his wife's face imprinted in the plant matter. This was the origin of corn, which fed the Abenaki for thousands of years. The story's implication seems to be that an earth goddess or fairylike spirit incarnated in human form in order to offer herself as a sacrificial gift to the Abenaki. In some versions of the story, she's called Corn Mother.

The identification of plants such as sweet flag and corn with particular spirits is a unique aspect of Abenaki folklore. Although stories in European fairy lore do associate fairies with features of the land such as marshes and mounds and with trees such as hawthorns, the idea that a plant itself could be a spirit (or descend from one) seems to be uniquely Abenaki. Even more foreign to European fairy lore is the notion that a supernatural being, apparently clothed in human flesh, could sacrifice herself so bloodily to produce food for the people to eat.

SUMMARY OF THE FAIRY CENSUS FOR VERMONT

The Fairy Census of 2017–2023 includes the testimony of three Vermont residents. Two of the responses follow the familiar pattern of describing fairies as "spheres" or "balls" of light and as flashes of color. The first respondent, a woman in her fifties, was walking in a wood that she described as a "haunted forest" when a hundred or so "cylindrical" and "glass-like" bodies of light revealed themselves to her. These cylindrical bodies were speckled, as if containing "energetic filaments." The woman watched the lights for many hours in the lead up to midnight and then went home.

The second response came from a teenage girl who described seeing a "glowing flash of white" in the hallway of a private home. This was followed by the appearance of "faintly glowing yellow wings," which she likened to a "butterfly." Although the girl couldn't describe the fairy in detail, the momentary appearance of "yellow wings" made a strong impression on her mind.

These descriptions, in which the fairies appear to be beings of light, strongly agree with encounters related elsewhere in the census for New England. In keeping with those descriptions, the respondents were also female.

The final response is perhaps the most vivid and concrete, for the woman in question (in her twenties and walking in woodlands) clearly saw a hunched human-sized figure "completely covered" in a brown cloak with what looked like roots on it. The woman claimed to have seen many fairies and spirits in the woodland where she was walking, not all of them friendly beings, but this one put her immediately "at ease." The encounter lasted only a few seconds, but it felt like a pause in time. She wondered if the being was the spirit of one of the trees along the trail. "I felt with certainty [that] what I saw was a fairy," she wrote.

This last encounter is unusual in the census findings for New England in that the fairy had a human-like size and appearance.

CONCLUSION

I t's clear from the preceding chapters that New England's Puritan culture didn't stop fairy folklore from arriving in the region with the many immigrants who came here between the seventeenth and nineteenth centuries. We've seen evidence of early belief in fairies among English, Irish, French Canadian and Scots Irish immigrants. While accounts of fairy encounters from colonial America are not exactly forthcoming, the descendants of immigrants from that period have left us living reminders of their beliefs. Although the records are sporadic, suggesting fairy folklore wasn't exactly ubiquitous in New England, the number of stories we've managed to collect is rather surprising, especially considering the cultural environment in which those immigrants lived. The early English who believed in fairies faced great opposition to their beliefs from the dominant Puritan culture, while Irish immigrants in later years faced the Catholic Church's general opposition to superstition and their own desire to fit into the Yankee-dominant culture. Such pressures encouraged immigrants to abandon Old World beliefs. Where immigrants managed to hold on to their beliefs and successfully pass down stories to subsequent generations, it was usually because they'd settled in areas relatively free from such influences. This included places like Marblehead, which embraced a more liberal culture, and isolated areas such as northern Maine, largely populated by Acadians and other French Canadians.

On the whole, it should be admitted that Americans tended to prefer stories about other supernatural beings to stories about fairies. This includes stories about witches, ghosts, the devil and even vampires. They often transferred to these beings traits and behaviors that in Europe had once been associated with fairies, including a hatred of iron and interference in farming and culinary activities. The nineteenth-century folklore of Vermont perfectly demonstrates the American preference for witches over fairies. While no historical stories about European fairies seem to have survived in Vermont (possibly because the population has always been so much smaller than other New England states), plenty of stories can be found about witches and vampires from the eighteenth and nineteenth century. One story from Orleans County involved a farmer who couldn't make his cream turn into butter no matter how much he churned it. Concluding the problem was the result of witchcraft, he shot his musket into the butter and was pleased to see the butter begin to form. Another witch story, from Shaftesbury, Vermont, concerned a horse that kept balking, leading the local people to conclude it had been bewitched. When they placed a red-hot horseshoe on the horse's hoof, the witch who'd performed the enchantment received a terrible burn to her foot. Such stories demonstrate that even when fairies cannot be found, the folklore associated with them is often present.

SPIRITUALISM AND FAIRY BELIEF

A word should be said here about the role of spiritualism in New England in the nineteenth century. One might well ask why belief in fairies was relatively sporadic when spiritualism—visions of ghosts, mediumship and attempts to communicate with the dead—was so widespread. This is properly a question for someone more knowledgeable in the history of spiritualism and its connection with other types of folklore. Nevertheless, folklorist Peter Muise has drawn attention to a strange connection between spiritualism and fairy lore from the 1840s: the story of a servant girl called Mary Jane who lived in Wrentham, Massachusetts. Under the influence of a spiritualist physician called Dr. Larkin, Mary Jane found herself possessed by spirits she identified as "fairies." These fairies included an "exceedingly beautiful" female fairy called Katy (whom Mary Jane considered to be her guardian angel), a group of friendly German fairies and a foul-mouthed spirit called Captain Goodhue, whom Mary Jane identified as "king of the fairies." Perhaps most significantly, Muise pointed out that the servant girl herself had been raised in Nova Scotia, a location steeped in the fairy lore of Scottish, Irish

Harriet Beecher Stowe, who, like her husband, had visions of fairies as a young person and also practiced spiritualism. *Public domain.*

and French immigrants. It's possible Mary Jane, a Nova Scotian by birth, interpreted the possessing spirits associated with spiritualism as "fairies," an appellation not found elsewhere in the history of spiritualism.

Another notable overlap between the spiritualist movement and belief in fairies can be seen in the example of two nineteenth-century Americans who took an active interest in spiritualism and reported fairy visions: the famous author of *Uncle Tom's Cabin*, Harriet Beecher Stowe, who grew up in Litchfield, Connecticut; and her husband Calvin Ellis Stowe, who lived in Massachusetts for most of his early life.

Although skeptical of what she called the "frivolity and worthlessness" of much of the spiritualist movement, Harriet Beecher Stowe became increasingly interested in séances following the death of her son Henry in 1857 and even spoke with a medium who channeled Henry's spirit. A woman of deep imagination and fervent religion, Stowe also grew up seeing fairies, as a contemporary biography of the author explained. Whether these fairies were projections of her imagination or genuine visions is not entirely clear. Nevertheless, Stowe saw many things as a child at her Litchfield home, including a "tiny woman clothed in white" emerging from a grove beside a lake and, following the woman, a "misshapen dwarf."

Stowe's visions pale in comparison to the richness of visions her husband experienced as a young man. Calvin Ellis Stowe, like his wife, had an active interest in spiritualism and worked with clergymen and professors who kept an open mind on the subject. He was quite the young visionary and saw many strange fairylike beings in South Natick, where he grew up. As he recounted in an 1834 spiritual autobiography, he first started seeing spirits with a "human form but under a shadowy outline that seemed just ready to melt into air." These progressed to more elaborate visions, including one of a woman, about eight inches tall, wearing a black robe. Finally, he saw a whole company of fairies dancing on his windowsill, including a king and queen who were slightly larger than the rest and bore a scepter and crown. Although the fairies smiled at Stowe, he described their faces as having a kind of "sinister and selfish expression" that stopped him from trusting them completely. The similarity between Stowe's visions and those of his wife are quite striking, and one can't help wondering if the pair bonded over them. What should we make of the connection between the Stowes' spiritualism and their fairy encounters? The topic is certainly worth exploring further.

FAIRIES, ANCIENT AND MODERN

One of the most fascinating aspects of New England's fairy folklore is the sheer variety of influences to be found. The most ancient traditions are, of course, those of the various Indigenous peoples who live here. Fairylike beings can be found in the folklore of all the Native American tribes, and as we've seen, they fall into different categories such as Little People, water fairies, underwater-dwelling dwarves, swamp spirits and mountain spirits. Many Indigenous stories about these beings seem to have arisen from a desire on the part of the Algonquian people to understand unexplainable phenomena. They used stories of supernatural beings to explain various facts of life, including geological processes, natural dangers, the appearance of swamps, disappearance of tribal members, the powers of shamanism, sickness and medicine. They also told stories to educate young people, pass on important values, protect the community from danger and maintain social cohesion. In the process, they left a treasury of myths and legends, even more fascinating because they're tied to specific locations throughout New England, many of them extremely beautiful.

A word should be said here about modern fairy folklore, which is no less present in New England than the time-honored stories of Native American tribes. As the Fairy Censuses show, the fairy faith appears to be alive and well in New England, at least among a minority of residents. The evidence suggests that fairy experiences are more common among women than men. Although men do appear in the censuses for New England, they're found in fewer numbers; this could be because men have fewer experiences, choose not to share their experiences or interpret their encounters differently. A majority of the visions reported in the censuses take the form of bright, floating lights or shimmering humanoid beings with wings. While these are quite different from the Indigenous Little People of New England and also from the fairies of British and Irish lore, they appear to be the most common type of fairy seen in the Northeast today.

Besides the censuses, evidence suggests that other types of fairy folklore have developed in recent years. This includes word-of-mouth stories about malicious elves or fairies who drive people to madness at the site of the Little People's Village in Middlebury, Connecticut, and encounters with pukwudgies in Massachusetts' Freetown State Forest. It should be noted, however, that in the latter case, people's descriptions of these beings have little in common with the Indigenous folklore about them. Reporting of pukwudgie sightings seems to have undergone a snowball effect in recent years, as similar stories about hikers and dog walkers encountering the beings have emerged. While these stories are interesting in themselves—representing a new type of folklore—care should be taken when publicizing them not to overshadow or warp authentic Indigenous traditions.

Another type of modern New England folklore about fairies can be seen in "campfire tales" or urban legends. These are stories told for entertainment, usually having little basis in historical fact and often debunked by the relevant authorities. Nevertheless, they do represent an oral tradition about fairies, closer to ghost stories than attested folklore. I've generally chosen not to include this type of tale in the book, but I believe that one, in particular, is worth sharing, as it concerns an important feature of fairy folklore: the fairy changeling.

The story takes place at Mount Holyoke College, the prestigious nineteenth-century women's college in South Hadley, Massachusetts. Although the archivist at Mount Holyoke appears to have debunked most of the scary stories set on campus, this one has circulated in the college's residence halls for many years, taking various forms, and has not yet been debunked. The story centers on a dormitory called Pearsons Annex, a Colonial-style home built in 1810 (originally called the Brick Store). According to legend, at the beginning of the nineteenth century, a young Irish immigrant couple lived in the building with their newborn baby. The woman came from a superstitious Irish family with a history of believing in ghosts and fairies. When her husband began to have an affair, she noticed he was missing from the home a lot and became extremely anxious. At the same time, the woman's baby wouldn't stop crying and never seemed happy. Its appetite was enormous, and she could never sate it.

All this convinced the woman that fairies had stolen her baby and had left a fairy changeling in its place; the reason the child wouldn't stop crying, she said, was because it didn't belong to her at all. Such beliefs are attested in nineteenth-century Ireland and were sometimes used to explain child health conditions: if a child developed a disorder later in childhood, people said the fairies must have stolen the child and left behind a fairy baby. Not only did the woman believe her baby was a fairy, but she also became convinced her husband was a changeling, his absences from home being evidence of his dalliances in the Land of Fae. One night, the husband returned home to find his wife had murdered their baby. The woman stated she believed her real baby would soon return. She then attacked her husband, who was able to fight her off. During the struggle, he stabbed her through the chest. The story goes that the man went mad and was placed in an asylum.

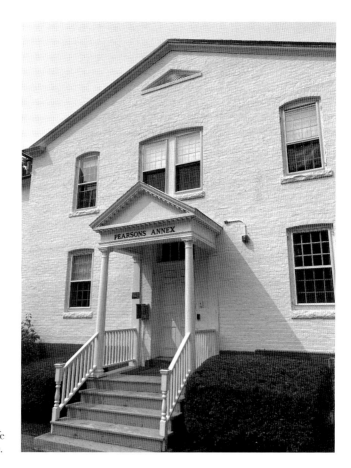

Pearsons' Annex, hall of residence at Mount Holyoke College, setting for a horrific fairy-changeling legend that echoed a real-life murder. *Author's photo.*

The tale is a gruesome one and is easy to dismiss as having no basis in reality. In fact, the earliest version of the story, recorded in the 1970s, doesn't refer to a changeling at all, being much closer to a simple ghost story. However, the addition of a fairy changeling to the tale may have been inspired by a real-life case of a fairy changeling murder reported in a March 1863 edition of the *New York Times*, which also involved an Irishwoman and her baby. That case involved a thirty-eight-year-old woman called Mary Nell who lived with her husband, Mathias, and three-year-old son, John, in Manhattan's Upper West Side. Five months prior to the event, Mathias had been due to leave New York with his regiment to join the Civil War defenses of Washington, D.C. A matter of days before the regiment left, he deserted and returned to his wife and son. Mathias later shared he feared his wife was insane because she acted so strangely, which may have been his inducement to desert from the army. In the lead-up to the event, a man who formerly lived in the Nells' building on Eighty-Third Street (between Eleventh and Twelfth Avenue) claimed that fairies were haunting the residence, and Mary became convinced her child was a changeling. Irish superstitions had taught her that one way to drive out a fairy changeling was to place the child on a red-hot shovel. If the child was indeed a changeling, the fairy would fly away, leaving behind the original child. Sadly, Mary placed young John on a heated shovel and inflicted such bad burns he died within a week. Committed to the New York City Lunatic Asylum, she later lived as a widow in Manhattan.

It seems to me that the changeling version of the Mount Holyoke story most likely originated in the case of Mary Nell. At some point in time, as various stories circulated around the Mount Holyoke campus, someone may have mixed up the original ghost story with a Mary Nell–inspired story of a changeling murder, thereby leaving us with the composite story we have today.

An example of fairy folklore's darkest aspect, the tale is certainly the most gruesome and tragic story I've investigated for this book. As for Mary Nell, how should we understand her story? It seems to me that three interpretations are possible. The first interpretation—that Mary Nell's judgment was unclouded and that her baby had really been taken from her—risks trivializing the fate of the poor child, John, at the heart of the events. The second interpretation—that Mary Nell suffered from a psychotic illness—implies that ideas associated with fairy folklore had become attached to Mary's illness but were secondary to the illness itself. The third interpretation—that Mary was sane and that her beliefs had seriously misled her—perhaps serves as a warning of what can happen when fairy folklore becomes totally unmoored from reality.

I'll leave it up to the reader to decide which interpretation they consider to be most likely.

A GLOSSARY OF
NEW ENGLAND FAIRIES

ALOMBEGWINOSIS
Dwarves whose name means "underwater man-dwarf." They live in deep pools in Maine's Penobscot River, especially opposite Indian Island in Milford and Lincoln Island, forty miles north. Two feet tall. Brown in color. Their appearance is a premonition that someone will drown. Known to upset Penobscot canoes. Have magical powers and can grant wishes.

BANSHEE
Female fairy whose name means "fairy woman." Seen in Harrisville, Rhode Island. Attached to Irish American families. Her wail foretells the death of a family member.

BOGLES
Goblin-like fairy of Scottish and Northern English origin found in Marblehead, Massachusetts. Known to snatch people walking home at twilight.

CORN MOTHER
A beautiful magical woman or earth goddess known to Maine's Penobscot people. She created corn through an act of self-sacrifice so the Penobscot could eat.

FEU FOLLET

A fire sprite found in Maine, usually seen as a lick of flame that floats over water or land. It sometimes chases people, especially when provoked.

GNOMES

Little People seen by Dora Kunz in the New Hampshire woodlands. Brown and gold in color.

GRANNY SQUANNIT

Medicine woman derived from a women's deity called Squauanit, meaning "woman spirit." She lives on Mohegan Hill, Cape Cod and Martha's Vineyard. Leader of the makiawisug. She heals tribe members and the Little People with herbs. Covers her face with her long hair. Steals naughty children.

HOBGOBLIN

A type of mischievous household goblin originating in English folklore and found in Marblehead, Massachusetts.

LUTIN

A gnomelike French fairy or goblin found in northern Maine, especially in Aroostook County's St. John Valley. Likes to braid horses' manes and stop cream from solidifying into butter. He enters homes to disrupt daily household activities.

MAKIAWISUG

Little People who live on Mohegan Hill, Connecticut. Their name may be derived from the words for moccasin and whip-poor-will. About two feet tall. They wear moccasin-flower shoes and can make themselves invisible by pointing at someone. They receive offerings from the Mohegans and take the form of wild animals.

MANOGEMASSAK

Water fairies found in Vermont whose name means "Little People." They travel in stone canoes, have thin faces like axe blades and speak in squeaky voices. They're thought to make the button-like stone concretions found in Button Bay on Lake Champlain. Probably synonymous with oonohgamesuk and wenagameswook.

Marten

A mikummwess companion or adopted younger brother of Glooskap. His name is Apistanewj in the Algonquian language. He usually takes the form of a youth but can also turn himself into a baby, little boy or man. He sometimes takes the form of a marten, a type of weasel. He eats from a birchbark dish and wears Glooskap's belt, giving him magical powers.

Maski'ksu

A woman with very dark skin, two and a half feet tall, whose name means "toad creature." She's found in northern New England and resides in swamps and forests near Native American settlements. She longs to hold men and children, but her touch causes death.

Mikummwessuk

Little People or wood spirits who live in Maine. Glooskap created them before he made humans. They act as familiars to shamans and bestow magical powers. Although they can be opposed to humans, they may also be very friendly. They're usually invisible, seen only by witches and shamans. They may seduce women and lure them into the woods. Among the Maliseets of northern Maine, Mikumwesu was a powerful dwarf and brother of Glooskap.

Mountain Spirits

Live in New Hampshire's White Mountains and appear in human form. Believed to take human lovers from among the Abenaki people.

Nagumwasuk

Ugly sprites who live near the Passamaquoddy in Maine. Friendly. Possibly synonymous with wenagameswook.

Oonohgamesuk

Little People whose name is translated variously as "water fairies", "elves", "sprites" or "water goblins." They live in the low-lying tract of land beside the Saco River and at Diana's Baths near North Conway, both in New Hampshire. They also live around Mount Katahdin in Maine and in the Lake Champlain Valley in Vermont. May torment people with arrows or darts. Among the first beings to be created by Glooskap, before humans. Probably synonymous with manogemassak and wenagameswook.

PIXIES

Mischievous and malicious fairies who live underground in Marblehead, Massachusetts. They like to lead people astray at night. One must turn an item of clothing inside out to guard against their enchantment.

PUKWUDGIES

Little People who live in the marshes around Popponesset Bay on Cape Cod. Later thought to inhabit the Freetown State Forest and Hockamock Swamp. They are often depicted as gray, knee high, with porcupine-style quills. They like to torment humans with darts, play tricks on them or push them off cliffs. They may take the form of wild animals.

SKWAKOWTEMUS

Female swamp spirit whose name means Swamp Woman. She lives in the swamps of northern New England and wears moss and bark for clothes. She has long mossy hair. Her touch kills children. Under the name Pskegdemus, she may be the ghost of a woman who died childless and now longs for male company.

SWAMP SPIRITS

Malicious spirits who live in Vermont's swamps. They cry out from the swamp grasses and steal or drown children who stray too close to the swamp.

TSIENNETO

A fairy queen who lives in Beaver Lake in Derry, New Hampshire. Associated with water and could travel up the Merrimack River. She likes to help people in distress.

WATER FAIRIES

Live in pools along brooks and in lakes. They may live along Greenwoods Brook in Sherman, Connecticut. Dora Kunz saw them as translucent pale-blue beings.

WENAGAMESWOOK

Water fairies or rock fairies found in Maine. They have narrow faces with large, aquiline noses. They sometimes warn Penobscot tribe members of threats such as approaching Mohawks. They travel by canoe along the Penobscot River and occasionally kidnap girls to marry them. They also kidnap children who stray into dangerous places. They're organized into twelve tribes, each having a king who ate Penobscot children. Probably synonymous with oonohgamesuk and manogemassak.

WOOD FAIRIES

Live in woodlands all over New England. Green in color. Body like gas. Help plants and flowers grow. Dora Kunz saw them in the New Hampshire woodlands.

WOOD NYMPH

Fairy who lives beside Beaver Lake in Derry, New Hampshire, according to a pamphlet by R.N. Richardson. Gray-colored and old. She hides in a Jack-in-the-pulpit flower.

SOURCES

Abelson, Jacqueline. "Mount Holyoke Ghost Stories." Jacqueline Abelson. October 16, 2017. http://www.jacquelineabelson.com/blog/mount-holyoke-ghost-stories

Allen, Eleanor P. "Harriet Beecher Stowe." *Lippincott's Monthly Magazine*, July–December 1890.

Bayliss, Clara Kern. "Witchcraft." *Journal of American Folklore* 21, no. 82 (1908): 363. https://doi.org/10.2307/534585.

Beaudoin, Richard. Student paper on French Canadian folklore. Northeast Archives of Folklore and Oral History, NA0455, 1968.

Bendici, Ray. "Little People's Village, Middlebury." Damned Connecticut. Accessed May 28, 2023. https://www.damnedct.com/little-peoples-village-middlebury/

Bridge Farmer, Sarah. "Folk-Lore of Marblehead, Mass." *Journal of American Folklore* 7, no. 26 (1894): 252–53.

Briggs, Katharine. *An Encyclopedia of Fairies*. New York: Pantheon Books, 1976.

Carder H. Whaley. "The Hills of Matunuck." Paper printed by the Friends of the Robert Beverly Hale Library, Matunuck, RI, 2016.

Citro, Joseph. *Passing Strange*. Boston: Houghton Mifflin Company, 1996.

———. *Weird New England*. New York: Sterling Publishing Company, 2005.

Clough, Ben C. "Legends of Chappaquiddick." *Journal of American Folklore* 31, no. 122 (1918): 553–54.

Cormier, Geraldine. Student paper on French Canadian folklore. Northeast Archives of Folklore and Oral History, NA0081, 1965.

Eckstorm, Fannie Hardy. "'Pixilated,' a Marblehead Word." *American Speech* 16, no. 1 (1941): 78–80.

Evans Wentz, W.Y. *The Fairy-Faith in Celtic Countries*. London: Henry Frowde, 1911.

"Fairies and Elves: A History (as Read by Bill Cullina at the Fairy House Village Opening)." Coastal Maine Botanical Gardens. August 28, 2013. https://www.mainegardens.org/blog/fairies-and-elves-a-history-as-read-by-bill-cullina-at-the-fairy-house-village-opening.

Federal Writers' Project. *Connecticut: A Guide to Its Roads, Lore, and People*. Boston: Houghton Mifflin Company, 1938.

Fritz, Jean. *The Good Giants and the Bad Pukwudgies*. New York City: Putnam, 1982.

Hand, Wayland D. "European Fairy Lore in the New World." *Folklore* 92, no. 2 (1981): 141–48.

Haviland, William A., and Marjory W. Power. *The Original Vermonters*. Hanover, NH: University Press of New England, 1994.

Hawthorne, Nathaniel. *The Scarlet Letter*. Boston: Ticknor, Reed, and Fields, 1850.

Heffernan, Maureen. *Fairy Houses of the Maine Coast*. Camden, ME: Down East, 2010.

Holmes, Richard. "Tales of Old Derry: The Legend of the Derry Fairy." *Derry News*, November 13, 2008. https://www.derrynews.com/opinion/tales-of-old-derry-the-legend-of-the-derry-fairy/article_7e1d2749-daf8-5bd6-b474-1efe050a4890.html

Hunt Sterry, Iveagh, and William H. Garrigus. *They Found a Way: Connecticut's Restless People*. Brattleboro, VT: Stephen Daye Press, 1938.

Julyan, Robert, and Mary Julyan. *Place Names of the White Mountains*. Hanover, NH: University Press of New England, 1993.

Kirk, Robert. *The Secret Commonwealth of Elves, Fauns, and Fairies*. London: David Knutt, 1893.

Kruse, John T. *Faery: A Guide to the Lore, Magic, and World of the Good Folk*. Woodbury, MN: Llewellyn Publications, 2020.

Lawrence, Robert F. *The New Hampshire Churches*. Claremont, NH: Office of the Claremont Power-Press. 1856.

Leland, Charles G. *The Algonquin Legends of New England*. Boston: Houghton Mifflin and Company, 1884.

Macnab Currier, John. "Shooting Witches in Cream." *Journal of American Folklore* 6, no. 20 (1893): 70.

McKenna, Ray. "1854: An Irish Sojourner Visits Providence, Rhode Island." Federal Hill Irish. February 22, 2019. https://federalhillirish.com/f/1854-an-irish-sojourner-visits-providence-rhode-island

———. "Harrisville, Rhode Island: A Sanctuary for Ireland's Banished." Federal Hill Irish. June 14, 2020. https://federalhillirish.com/f/harrisville-rhode-island-a-sanctuary-for-irelands-banished

———. "The Wee People Amongst Us: From the Writings of Rose Shaw." Federal Hill Irish. December 13, 2021. https://federalhillirish.com/f/rose-shaw-ii-the-fairies-are-everywhere

Morse Earle, Alice. *In Old Narragansett*. New York: Charles Scriber's Sons, 1898.

Muise, Peter. "Foul-Mouthed Fairies and Spirit Possession in 1846." *New England Folklore*. October 19, 2016. https://newenglandfolklore.blogspot.com/2016/10/foul-mouthed-fairies-and-spirit.html

———. "Puritans and Pukwudgies." In *Magical Folk: British and Irish Fairies: 500 AD to the Present*, edited by Simon Young and Ceri Houlbrook. London: Gibson Square, 2022.

Nabokov, Peter. *Where the Lightning Strikes*. London: Penguin, 2006.

New York Times. "A Remarkable Case of Hallucination." March 18, 1863.

Ofgang, Erik. "The Truth Behind a Mysterious 'Fairy' Village in the Woods Along I-84." CT Insider. February 18, 2020. https://www.ctinsider.com/connecticutmagazine/news-people/article/The-truth-behind-a-mysterious-fairy-village-in-17045120.php

Packard, Christopher. *Mythical Creatures of Maine*. Camden, ME: Down East Books, 2021.

Philips, David E. *Legendary Connecticut: Traditional Tales from the Nutmeg State*. Evanston, IL: Northwestern University Press, 1995.

Reynard, Elizabeth. *The Narrow Land: Folk Chronicles of Old Cape Cod*. Boston: Houghton Mifflin, 1968.

Richardson, R.N. "Tsienneto: A Legend of Beaver Lake." Self-published, pamphlet, 1907.

Roads, Samuel. *The History and Traditions of Marblehead*. Boston: Houghton, Osgood, and Company, 1880.

Robinson Hazard, Thomas. *The Jonny-Cake Papers of Shepherd Tom*. Boston: Merrymount Press, 1915.

Russell Emerson, Ellen. *Indian Myths, or Legends, Traditions, and Symbols of the Aborigines of America*. Boston: James R. Osgood and Company, 1884.

Santiago, Ellyn. "Mohegan Tribe's Cultural Boundary Reduced But Still Could Block Affordable Housing." Patch. September 24, 2012. https://patch.com/connecticut/montville-ct/mohegan-tribe-s-cultural-boundary-reduced-but-still-cf43f7b1f78

Sawyer Lord, Priscilla, and Virginia Clegg Gamage. *Marblehead: The Spirit of '76 Lives Here*. Boston: Chilton Book Company, 1972.

Sayet, Rachel. "Moshup's Continuance: Sovereignty and the Literature of the Land in the Aquinnah Wampanoag Nation." Master's thesis, Harvard University Extension School, 2012.

Schoolcraft, Henry. *The Myth of Hiawatha and Other Oral Legends, Mythologic and Allegoric, of the North American Indians*. Philadelphia: J.B. Lippincott & Company, 1856.

Sherman Sentinel. "The Way We Were." May 7, 1993.

Simmons, William S. *Spirit of the New England Tribes: Indian History and Folklore*. Hanover, NH: University Press of New England,1986.

Skinner, Charles M. *Myths and Legends of Our Own Land*. Philadelphia: J.P. Lippincott Company, 1896.

Speare, Eva A. *More New Hampshire Folk Tales*. Printed for the author, 1936.

———. *New Hampshire Folk Tales*. Canaan, NH: Phoenix Publishing, 1974.

Speck, Frank G. "Penobscot Tales and Religious Beliefs." *Journal of American Folklore* 48, no. 187 (1935): 1–107.

Stamp, Harley. "The Water-Fairies." *Journal of American Folklore* 28, no. 109 (1915): 310–16.

Story, William Wetmore. *Life and Letters of Joseph Story*. London: John Chapman, 1851.

Stowe, Charles E. *Life of Harriet Beecher Stowe*. Boston: Houghton Mifflin, 1890.

Thomas, Peter A. February 19, 2023. "The Sokokis and Their World in 1663." Talk on the occasion of the 350th Anniversary Celebrations of Northfield, Vermont.

Tregarthen, Enys. *Pixie Legends and Folklore*. Avenel, NJ: Gramercy Books, 1995.

Van Gelder, Dora. *The Real World of Fairies*. Wheaton, IL: Quest Books, 1999.

Violette, Claire. Student paper on French Canadian folklore. Northeast Archives of Folklore and Oral History, NA0475, 1968.

Walker, Willard. "Wabanaki 'Little People' and Passamaquoddy Social Control." Papers of the 27th Algonquian Conference. ed. David H. Pentland. University of Manitoba Press: Winnipeg, 1996.

Williams, Roger. *A Key Into The Language of America*. London: Gregory Dexter, 1643.

Wilson, Julius. "Perry, Marthy, and 'Honeymug.'" Unpublished manuscript, 1961, typescript.

Wilson, Margaret. "Wanzers: A Sketch by Margaret Wilson Lund." Unpublished manuscript, n.d., typescript.

Woodyard, Chris. "Banshees and Changelings." In *Magical Folk: British and Irish Fairies: 500 AD to the Present*, edited by Simon Young and Ceri Houlbrook. London: Gibson Square, 2022.

Woodyard, Chris, and Simon Young. "Three Notes and a Handlist of North American Fairies." *Supernatural Studies* 6, no. 1 (2019): 56–85.

Young, Simon. "The Fairy Census 2014–2017." Fairyist. January 8, 2018. https://www.fairyist.com/wp-content/uploads/2014/10/The-Fairy-Census-2014-2017-1.pdf

———. "Pixilated, a Somerset Word?" *Tradition Today* 7 (2018): 79–80

ABOUT THE AUTHOR

Andrew Warburton grew up in Bristol, England. He received his master's in creative writing at Bath Spa University and has published poems and short stories. He lived in Massachusetts for many years and now lives in Rhode Island. *New England Fairies* is his first book. He blogs about fairies at fairiesofnewengland.com.

Visit us at
www.historypress.com